Competitive Intelligence

Jim Underwood

STRATEGY

03.09

- ■ Fast track route to mastering the art of competitor intelligence

- ■ Covers the fundamentals of competitor intelligence, from securing CEO buy-in and making sure the right people are in place to creating an internal intelligence system and setting up a war room

- ◀ Examples and lessons from some of the world's most intelligent businesses, including Motorola and Apple, and ideas from the smartest thinkers including Jan Herring, Ben Gilad and Leonard Fuld

- ◀ Includes a glossary of key concepts and a comprehensive resources guide

>>EXPRESS EXEC.COM<<

essential management thinking at your fingertips

Copyright © Capstone Publishing 2002

The right of Jim Underwood to be identified as the author of this work has been
asserted in accordance with the Copyright, Designs and Patents Act 1988

First published 2002 by
Capstone Publishing (a Wiley company)
8 Newtec Place
Magdalen Road
Oxford OX4 1RE
United Kingdom
http://www.capstoneideas.com

CIP catalogue records for this book are available from the British Library and the
US Library of Congress

ISBN 1-84112-226-2

Printed and bound in Great Britain

This book is printed on acid-free paper

Substantial discounts on bulk quantities of Capstone books are available
to corporations, professional associations and other organizations. Please
contact Capstone for more details on +44 (0)1865 798 623 or (fax) +44
(0)1865 240 941 or (e-mail) info@wiley-capstone.co.uk

Contents

Introduction to ExpressExec

ExpressExec is 3 million words of the latest management thinking compiled into 10 modules. Each module contains 10 individual titles forming a comprehensive resource of current business practice written by leading practitioners in their field. From brand management to balanced scorecard, ExpressExec enables you to grasp the key concepts behind each subject and implement the theory immediately. Each of the 100 titles is available in print and electronic formats.

Through the ExpressExec.com Website you will discover that you can access the complete resource in a number of ways:

» printed books or e-books;
» e-content – PDF or XML (for licensed syndication) adding value to an intranet or Internet site;
» a corporate e-learning/knowledge management solution providing a cost-effective platform for developing skills and sharing knowledge within an organization;
» bespoke delivery – tailored solutions to solve your need.

Why not visit www.expressexec.com and register for free key management briefings, a monthly newsletter and interactive skills checklists. Share your ideas about ExpressExec and your thoughts about business today.

Please contact elound@wiley-capstone.co.uk for more information.

Introduction to
Expression

Introduction

This chapter discusses the importance of intelligence and how it can directly impact a company's profit.

In describing companies, two terms are often used to explain key differences: *closed system* and *open system*. A closed system is one that is internally focused and does not generally respond to external change. An open system is one that uses external information to drive organizational change.

Generally, closed systems do not last long in turbulent environments. Conversely, open systems are able to be highly adaptive, and therefore tend to be able to achieve long-term sustainable profitability. At the heart of sustainable profitability is an organization's ability to learn. That is why the gathering of intelligence is so critical to the growth and survival of the firm.

A WORLD OF INTELLIGENCE

There are a number of words or phrases that are used to describe *competitive intelligence*. Some attempt to differentiate between *competitive intelligence*, *intelligence*, *business intelligence*, and *strategic intelligence*. In this book a great deal of effort will not be made to differentiate between the many definitions that have been proposed for each of these terms. Generally, the term *competitive intelligence* or simply *intelligence* will be used to represent the entire field of intelligence.

The *intelligence function* is defined and practiced in different ways at different companies. Ideally, the intelligence function at a company is a team of trained individuals who are given the task of assessing competitors and external forces for the purpose of preparing the company for future events and conditions. At some companies, the intelligence function is little more than a market research group. At others, it is comprised of senior executives who spend a great deal of their time learning about impending changes in the global industry.

In growing, adaptive companies, management's view of their role and the role of intelligence is quite different than that at non-adaptive companies. The reason is, whether explicit or not, that those at adaptive companies seem to have a different understanding of what management is and is not. As a result, the intelligence function is different from company to company.

In other books I have written, I have proposed that the definition of *management* should be changed. The currently popular definition is "planning, organizing, leading, and controlling." In the linear, predictable world of the 1940s or 1950s, that might have been an acceptable philosophy of management. The new world of the twenty-first century is far from being linear or predictable.

It is somewhat remarkable that so many books have been written about change, chaos, and uncertainty, yet no one has stopped to consider whether or not the above definition is really an appropriate philosophy to use as a basis for managing a company. I believe that *management* must be redefined to meet the times. Here is my definition: "Management is the leading of organizational learning, transformation, and performance."[1]

"What in the world," you might ask, "does a new definition of *management* have to do with *competitive intelligence*?" It has everything to do with competitive intelligence. Competitive intelligence has to do with changes in the future market. Understanding what already exists is of little value. The key is to be able to look at the world and to begin to understand what the world of the future will look like. That is where intelligence has its roots: organizational learning. Learning is the prolegomena of future profit. Organizational learning provides corporate management with the information to allow them to initiate organizational transformation that will adapt the firm to the future environment. Finally, if the organization has learned, and effectively been transformed, it will maximize performance.

Effective intelligence is the foundation of organizational learning. Absent an effective intelligence function, an organization is a closed system and has no roadmap to future profit. Intelligence is critical.

Companies gather intelligence in many different ways. At some companies, such as Texas Instruments, Inc., the senior executives of the firm are expected to spend much of their time learning about what the firm must become in the future. At others, the firm's culture sets expectations that encourage every employee to be a part of the learning/intelligence process. At still other companies, like Motorola, there are formal intelligence organizations that report directly to the senior executive of the firm. At numerous others, there are hybrid forms of all three approaches.

WINNERS ARE LEARNERS

Every year, a lot of books are written about executives of companies. The idea must be that other managers can read about this or that executive, and somehow learn how to be a better manager. It might be somewhat like a "best-practice" approach to looking at leadership. In a lot of cases, the books will talk about some of the bizarre behaviors that winning executives use to encourage their team to "get out of the box" in their approach to leading the company. A lot of these managers also understand the importance of competitive intelligence. But there is more.

Organizational success begins with learning. That is, it's all about knowledge. Knowledge about future markets, competitors' executive profiles, future competitor products, and numerous other areas is the foundation of the future of the organization. The heart of the development of knowledge is the corporate intelligence function. In some cases, that is not true. A lot of companies do not recognize the value of intelligence, so when an economic downturn hits the firm, the intelligence team is the first to be downsized. Still other companies have no intelligence function at all. They see no value in the function, and certainly cannot justify the financial outlay required for a professional intelligence function.

There are a number of points that need to be made at this time. First, if an organization is going to make a commitment to start an intelligence function, they need to understand the importance and the role of intelligence in the first place. Executives that cut the intelligence function as a cost-cutting opportunity simply do not realize the role that intelligence can play in the generation of future profit potential. Second, a lot of intelligence organizations do not do a lot of intelligence work. They buy reports. They search databases. That's about it. In a number of instances, I have personally seen companies form intelligence units, staff them with unqualified clerical-level workers, and wonder why they never got any value out of the intelligence department. Companies that form intelligence units need to hire and train the very best professionals they can find. If they do not, they deserve the outcome they achieve. Finally, unless the intelligence function reports directly to the CEO, in most cases it will always be subject to the whims of those using the budget-cutting ax.

FUTURE PROFIT POTENTIAL

Strategy is defined by H. Igor Ansoff as "creating future profit potential."[2] This definition reveals the profit-critical role of intelligence (and as a strategic partner) in the organization. Without appropriate knowledge about the future, future profit potential is diminished. It is just that simple. Intelligence is a bottom-line activity and must be treated as such. Companies that do not understand the role of professional intelligence will lack the ability to create future profit potential.

NOTES

1 Underwood, J.D. (2001) *Thriving in E-Chaos*. Prima Publishing, Roseville, CA.
2 Ansoff, H.I. and McDonnell, E.J. (1990) *Implanting Strategic Management*, 2nd edn. Prentice Hall International (UK), Hertfordshire.

What is Competitive Intelligence?

This chapter provides an introduction to the field of intelligence, including appropriate definitions.

Ask 10 people what *competitive intelligence* is, and more than likely 10 different answers will be given. In fact, competitive intelligence has numerous names at different companies, including *intelligence, business intelligence*, and in some cases the function is simply called *research*.

This is not a book for the intelligence technician. This is a book for managers who need to have a better understanding of the value and use of intelligence. It is hoped that by the end of the book, the reader will have a much more complete understanding as to how intelligence information can have a bottom-line impact on almost any organization.

DEFINING COMPETITIVE INTELLIGENCE

Intelligence involves bribery, espionage, illicit acquisition of information, legitimate information-gathering, analysis, and the presentation of intelligence information. Most who work in intelligence probably read the first sentence of this paragraph in shock. Because, more than likely, they do not define *intelligence* in the same way that the preceding sentence does.

In most cases, readers in many countries will define *competitive intelligence* in terms of the ethical standards involved in gathering intelligence. However, it is important for an individual who is responsible for an organization's intelligence function to understand that the world is not necessarily bound by your ethical standards. If the intelligence manager is also responsible for counter-economic espionage at the firm – they probably should be – then the first definition is much more appropriate. The nature of competitive intelligence, and the practices of some its practitioners, must be the concern of every senior manager at every firm.

At most North American and European firms, any definition of *competitive intelligence* will usually include a reference to the "ethical" acquisition of information. In most cases, this means that the intelligence analyst will not use bribery or deception in the gathering of information. With this understanding, it is appropriate to hazard a definition: "Competitive intelligence is the identification of strategically important corporate intelligence (knowledge) needs and the process of resolving those needs through ethical information-gathering, analysis, and the presentation of such analysis to clients (internal or external)."

In some organizations, intelligence-gathering and analysis is informal. In fact, many companies do not have a formal intelligence function. Generally, whether formal or informal, the intelligence process begins with the identification of a need. Next, decisions have to be made about how the information is to be gathered. In the simplest form, the information-gathering process may involve going to a trade show or getting a competitor's price list. Once gathered, the information must be analyzed. The analyst must take the information from a "What do you see?" to a "What does it mean?" stage. Information generally does not convey the "What does it mean?" message. That is where the human mind is critical. Finally, the analyst must take the information and communicate it. Often, the more dissonant the information (dissonance involves the difference between reality and people's mental models), the more difficult it is to get a meaningful response from the recipient of the analysis.

THE INTELLIGENCE CYCLE

Another way of developing an understanding of intelligence is a somewhat time-worn look at describing the process of intelligence. The planning cycle (Fig. 2.1) might serve as an approach to looking at intelligence in an extremely general manner, but the cycle does not reveal what the process is really all about, or should be all about.

Fig. 2.1   The planning cycle.

Consider the following look at the intelligence process. It is important to understand that the actual process is usually much more complex than this simple presentation (Fig. 2.2) suggests.

Need identification

Preliminary project definition

Preliminary (broad) research

Project redefinition

Research design

Data collection

Data analysis

Synthesis

Communicating the knowledge

Fig. 2.2 The intelligence process.

The intelligence analyst is limited by numerous constraints. Included in those constraints are time, project constraints, available funds, internal power (of the intelligence unit), internal politics, ethical standards, data quality, source quality, and source integrity. There are a number of others, but these are the most obvious. Needless to say, the intelligence analyst's job is further complicated by the fact that no two intelligence assignments are the same. The needs and challenges related to each project are almost always different. Time constraints alone can radically change every aspect of the intelligence process.

What is the purpose of competitive intelligence? It is not to create a competitive advantage. Competitive advantage has historically been based upon a hypothesis that a firm may somehow be able to differentiate itself based upon historic competencies. That idea has come under a great deal of criticism as of late, and for very good reason. It is a concept that is founded in linear thinking. The reality is that the world is just not linear. That is why competitive intelligence has become increasingly valuable in the new complex competitive environment of the twenty-first century.

In complex environments, successful firms do not simply find a success formula or a set of competencies and camp on them. Successful firms are dynamic and often non-linear in their behavior, just as the environment is non-linear. Successful firms in such environments are those that can continually discover competitive opportunities. It is the stream of competitive opportunities that allow an organization to continually renew itself in harmony with the competitive environment. Simply put: successful firms differentiate themselves from other firms by being continually different. Intelligence is the critical driver of information that will allow a firm to adapt pre-emptively to the future environment.

INTELLIGENCE GOES BY MANY NAMES

As suggested earlier, a lot of companies have intelligence functions but choose to call them research departments. Some might suggest that a number of very successful global enterprises do quite well without intelligence units. Those observations may not be very accurate.

One global technology firm makes no secret of the fact that they simply have no intelligence function. Discussions with senior executives reveal just the opposite – the firm's top 10 executives spend much of their time gathering intelligence. In fact, the senior executive team is expected to be traveling globally at least 60% of the time. In the opinion of those running this organization, it is the executives who must lead organizational learning if they are going to be able to drive change into the firm effectively. (Note: It is regrettable that the actual name of this firm cannot be revealed. They have consistently been one of the top global technology firms around for a number of years.)

THE IMPORTANCE OF COMPETITIVE INTELLIGENCE

Regardless of what it is called or how it is done, competitive intelligence is extremely important if a company is to stay ahead of its competition. Intelligence is the foundation of knowledge, which ultimately is the source of profit.

The Evolution of Intelligence

This chapter takes a look at the long, rich history of the practice of intelligence over the centuries.

Historical records reveal the important role that intelligence has played in the history of countries. Some might say that gathering intelligence is simply common sense. Yet, history is replete with instances in which leaders either failed to gather intelligence information or failed to heed it, once they had it. As the record indicates, the best intelligence in the world is useless if the person with the power is unwilling to listen. As a result, processes for managing change (and dissonant information) have become an important aspect of the intelligence process. In looking at the evolution of the field, history reveals a significant contrast. On the one hand, intelligence is still much the same as it has been for thousands of years. On the other, it is drastically different today than it has ever been. The box below represents the diversity of intelligence as it has been recorded over the last 3000 years.

A TIMELINE SHOWING THE EVOLUTION OF INTELLIGENCE

» **c. 1000 BC**: The practice of intelligence is evident in the earliest written records.
» **c.1000 AD**: Intelligence and the use of spies continue to play an important role in planning for battle.
» **1940s**: Intelligence becomes a critical aspect of military endeavors; electronic surveillance is introduced.
» **1960s**: Research emerges as an important aspect of understanding competitors.
» **1980s**: Numerous companies introduce formal business intelligence-gathering functions.
» **1980s**: The Japanese make extensive use of industrial espionage to acquire key technologies.
» **1990s**: Intelligence goes electronic; commercial databases become popular resources for business intelligence.
» **2000**: Intelligence goes complex; the corporate intelligence community recognizes the need for complexity-based intelligence methodologies and tools.

INTELLIGENCE: A NEED-BASED PROCESS

Almost 4000 years ago, a man named Moses was given the task of leading a small band of people into a land. Being a man of wisdom, Moses concluded that he needed to gather intelligence about the land before he committed the group's main battle force to the conquest. So he decided to send out spies to look at the land. When they returned, their story was not one of encouragement.

The spies reported that the land was one of heavily fortified cities. It would be extremely difficult, they concluded, for the small band to take on such barriers. There was one other problem. The soldiers in this land were not like the soldiers that Moses had to deploy. They were bigger in size.

The spies' reports were a discouragement. In fact, they were so discouraging that the people decided they were unwilling to follow Moses in any assault on this land. Finally, Moses decided not to proceed with the planned attack on the land.[1]

Having learned a lesson from Moses' failure, his successor Joshua resolved that he needed to approach things a little differently. He decided to send spies into the city of Jericho to gather intelligence about the same area that Moses had targeted. Being aware of Moses' previous problem, Joshua made sure that the spies were sent out secretly.

Once in the land, the spies found a willing co-conspirator in the person of Rahab. She was a prostitute by trade, but decided that she would assist the spies based upon the stories she had heard about the previous successes of Israel's fighting forces. She concealed the spies when their presence was detected, then sent their pursuers in the wrong direction when they tried to apprehend the spies.

Once back, the spies reported to Joshua. They described a land that was ripe for conquest. They described a people who did not have the confidence to face the people of Israel. Based upon their report, the decision was made to begin the assault on the land.[2]

The biblical story of the conquest of Canaan provides a great example of the history of intelligence. It also shows that not much has changed. People still try to gather information. Further, there is still disagreement as to what the information means. But none of the parties involved would disagree as to the value that the information contained.

A BASIS FOR GOOD DECISION-MAKING

When my father returned from serving overseas in the military, he brought with him a few dollars in foreign currency, which he immediately gave to me. The total value of the currency was probably less than $3. I was five years old at the time, and just had to show off my money to anyone who would listen. A group of older boys decided to play on the gullibility of a five-year-old, and convinced me that my small change was worth at least $1000. "In fact," they insisted, "you can go to the Jones store on the corner and they will cash it in for you." You can imagine the look of amusement on the proprietors' faces when this little kid brazenly walked through their front door, declaring that he wanted to exchange his valuable foreign currency for US dollars. That "lesson learned" has a lot of application in the intelligence arena. There are many things to consider when it comes to taking action based upon the input of others.

Intelligence has historically been about three things. First, it has been about gathering the right information from the right sources. Second, it has been about correctly analyzing the information. Third, it has been about getting others to take action on the basis of the intelligence. A good example of this is revealed in the events of the hours before the battle of the Little Bighorn.

General George Armstrong Custer was a renowned soldier. His reputation had grown to the point that when an opposing enemy force of Indians saw his uniform they would flee. This had held true until General Custer found himself facing a group of Indians at the Little Bighorn in Montana. There has been a lot of debate about what really happened to cause Custer's defeat. It is suggested that his failure to properly handle intelligence information may have had a lot to do with his demise.

It seems that General Custer's scouts began running into signs of enemy presence long before the fateful battle. In one case, the scouts reported, the Indians had crossed a river. The scouts were alarmed at what they saw. One crossing revealed that the group was so large that their tracks were a mile wide. That translates into a lot of Indians. In fact, it was the largest gathering of Indian tribes in the history of North America. And, as they say, "the rest is history."

As time progressed, the tools available for intelligence-gathering began to change. By World War I, manned balloons were used as stationary observation posts from which soldiers would attempt to look behind enemy lines to gather critical information about troop movements and deployments. Aircraft were also used for the same purposes. Through the various conflicts that followed, intelligence-gathering was becoming increasingly recognized for its importance to decision-making. The Gulf War conflict illustrates just how far technology had taken the field of intelligence by the 1990s. The allied powers had the ability to get information about every troop deployment throughout Kuwait and Iraq. The information allowed the allied forces to identify and target every key tactical unit that posed a threat.

INTELLIGENCE AND BUSINESS

Companies have always gathered intelligence. Whether it involved the simple act of looking at a competitor's pricing in a catalogue, or listening to a potential customer explain what they like about your competitor, intelligence-gathering in business is nothing new. Over time, the process has become more and more systematic. At a number of companies, formal research functions have been created. In some cases they are more marketing-oriented, but in others they are more comprehensive in nature.

Motorola's Bob Galvin recognized the need for effective intelligence when he initiated the formation of the firm's first intelligence group. Jan Herring, former CIA agent, was hired to develop the function for the firm. Over the years, the Motorola model has become the benchmark for companies wanting to create an intelligence function. At the same time, some companies realized that there was also a need to develop a counter-intelligence function. As a lot of companies appreciated that their new product developments had been compromised by less than scrupulous competitors, they understood that they had to be aggressive in protecting their secrets from competitors' intelligence initiatives.

INTELLIGENCE AND ETHICS

One of the first challenges that confronted companies engaging in the acquisition of intelligence had to do with ethics. The senior manager of an intelligence team in California tells the story of her experience in gathering intelligence in the 1980s. She said she had just called a major competitor and pretended to be a potential customer. She had carefully led the competitor's salesperson through a series of questions that revealed a great deal about the firm's pricing strategy and competitive positioning. She tells of how she got off the call and suddenly realized that she did not like the person she had become. She called the competitor back, apologized, and promised she would never again behave in a deceptive manner again.

The Society of Competitive Intelligence Professionals (SCIP) has developed a code of ethics for all of its members. It conveys the ethical standards that the society and its members agree to set as ethical standards for the gathering of intelligence. These are:

1 to continually strive to increase the recognition and respect of the profession;
2 to comply with all applicable laws, domestic and international;
3 to accurately disclose all relevant information, including one's identity and organization, prior to all interviews;
4 to fully respect all requests for confidentiality of information;
5 to avoid conflicts of interest in fulfilling one's duties;
6 to provide honest and realistic recommendations and conclusions in the execution of one's duties;
7 to promote this code of ethics within one's company, with third-party contractors, and within the entire profession;
8 to faithfully adhere to and abide by one's company policies, objectives, and guidelines.[3]

In spite of the professional code of ethics for the industry, there are those that do not play by these rules. The success of some global players in the acquisition of trade secrets by using unethical and often illegal means has encouraged others to follow suit.

This has created an entirely new industry of counter-espionage. Anthony McClure, a counter-espionage consultant for a number of major companies, suggests that the threat is growing: "In most cases, I find that I could penetrate a company's security in a matter of days and gain access to anything I want in short order." According to McClure, the use of very sophisticated technologies is common practice for a number of firms.

INTELLIGENCE AND TECHNOLOGY

In Chapter 6, the impact of technology upon the practice of intelligence is discussed at length. It is sufficient at this point simply to suggest that technology has changed the intelligence landscape. The emergence of the Internet, online databases, and the information explosion offers the intelligence profession an almost inexhaustible supply of data. In many cases, the information is so massive that the problem for the researcher is one of deciding how to manage the analysis of the information. In one project completed by this writer, a number of weeks were spent analyzing the information that had been obtained from a database search. After discarding the repetitive and less than relevant articles, there were still over 1500 articles that had to be dealt with.

INTELLIGENCE AND STRATEGY

As the process of developing corporate strategy becomes increasingly time- and information-sensitive, the value of an effective intelligence system is increasingly recognized. Both disciplines are sharing tools, and in many cases the process of gathering and analyzing data has become a seamless handoff to the strategy group. Further, those at executive level are developing an increasing appreciation of the value of good intelligence. The example set at companies like Motorola, Inc., has helped make the case for the value of intelligence.

CONCLUSION

Three factors are driving very rapid evolution in the field of intelligence. These are technology, soft systems, and value creation. The technological changes that will occur in the years 2002 to 2007 will be massive. The emergence of new soft systems (or non-linear systems) for assessing and analyzing intelligence will continue to improve. Finally, the value creation of the intelligence process itself is becoming apparent to all who operate in the new economy of uncertainty.

NOTES

1 Numbers 13, 14.
2 Joshua 2.
3 The SCIP code of ethics may be found at www.scip.org/ci/ethics.asp

The E-Dimension

The Internet has had a great deal to do with substantial changes in the practice of intelligence. This chapter takes a look at how the speed and quality of intelligence-gathering have been impacted.

The technology explosion of the 1990s and early 2000s has drastically changed the field of intelligence. Information that once took days or weeks to reach an analyst can now be obtained moments after an event has occurred. The simple act of conducting competitor research is now an entirely new process. The diffusion of technology and information has resulted in not only major changes in the speed at which intelligence can be gathered, but further it has multiplied the volume of information that is available. Truly, the e-dimension has changed the practice of intelligence.

LOOKING FOR DATA IN ALL THE RIGHT PLACES

In 1996, I was given a client assignment that involved the evolution of technologies. My task was to help the client understand where a certain technology would be three years in the future. In order to accomplish the task, I used the Ansoff turbulence model[1] as a basis for my work.

H. Igor Ansoff was quite well known in the 1960s and 1970s, but is not as well known today as he was then. He is the author of more than 100 articles and books on the topic of strategic management, and has been a leader in the development of long-term planning. He developed the *strategic success hypothesis* – of which the Ansoff turbulence model forms a part – which relates the performance of an organization with its ability to profile or match the competitive environment. His hypothesis has been validated in over 1000 studies of companies around the world, and is now called his *strategic success theory*. The following is a simplistic presentation of the actual model.

In using the Ansoff turbulence model, the researcher must first decide what future window in time will be studied. In the case of my client, industry churn was already quite turbulent, so the decision was made to focus upon the future in three years' time. The turbulence assessment is significantly more powerful than something like a SWOT (strengths, weaknesses, opportunities, and threats) analysis or a Five Forces analysis (see Chapter 6 for a fuller discussion of these analytical models). Here are three reasons why.

1 The turbulence assessment involves the future and not history or the present.

2 It is a non-linear tool (i.e. it does not assume the future is predictable).
3 It is a much more comprehensive tool.

Once completed, a turbulence analysis offers a great deal of insight into the future competitive environment. For example, with turbulence levels in excess of 3.5 on the scale (1 = low turbulence; 3 = moderate turbulence; 5 = high turbulence) we know that product life cycles are shortened, the number of competing technologies increases, and the value chain begins to undergo significant changes. At that level of turbulence, product pricing becomes increasingly commodity-based and generic strategies no longer work.

Here is the simplistic version of the Ansoff turbulence scale (Tables 4.1 and 4.2). In using the Ansoff turbulence scale, the researcher systematically investigates each related area until the level of future turbulence is determined. Then the value index for each item is combined to compute what is called future environmental turbulence.

Table 4.1 Future marketing turbulence.

Marketing behavior	Turbulence scale				
	1	2	3	4	5
Sales aggressiveness	Low		Moderate		High
Marketing aggressiveness	Low		Moderate		High
Marketing strategy	Serve customers		Grow market		Expand share
Industry capacity vs demand	Excess demand		Equilibrium		Excess capacity

Adapted with permission from H.I. Ansoff and E. McDonnell, *Implementing Strategic Management*, 2nd edn (Hertfordshire, Prentice Hall International (UK), 1990)

From a practice standpoint, three different views (or measurements) are obtained. First, if possible, a questionnaire is administered to the client firm to determine their managers' view of the future. Next, an

Table 4.2 Future innovation turbulence.

Innovation behavior	Turbulence scale				
	1	2	3	4	5
Innovation aggressiveness	Low		Moderate		High
Technological change	Slow		Moderate		Fast
Innovation strategy	Follower		Product improvement		Product innovation
Customer strategy	Meet needs		Stay close to customer		Anticipate unrealized needs
Product life cycles	Long		Moderate		Short

Adapted with permission from H.I. Ansoff and E. McDonnell, *Implementing Strategic Management*, 2nd edn (Hertfordshire, Prentice Hall International (UK), 1990)

extensive database investigation is conducted. The information is then overlaid on the turbulence model. Finally, a modified Delphi panel is utilized. Then, the researcher must analyze the differences between the three views in order to determine what the actual value is to be.

In the case of my project, I had a problem. My client needed to get some understanding of how technologies would change in his particular segment. The related decisions involved a lot of dollars. The project was further complicated by confusion in the minds of many of the experts I interviewed.

I expanded my database investigation in the hope of finding some shred of information that would help me find the answer I needed. I narrowed my search down to one specific competitor, and concluded that they held the key to how this technology was going to change. Finally, I discovered the text of a speech that had been given in New Zealand by one of the senior executives of the target firm. Yes, he had clearly laid out the company's strategy for that technology segment.

In this particular case, the availability of a global database proved invaluable to my investigation. Other clues emerged, which further affirmed the validity of the executive's statements. In the end, my access to the information enabled my client to get critical information at a fraction of the cost of what it would have been without the technical tools that were used.

THE INTERNET

The flood of information that hit the Internet in the late 1990s created a number of problems. For the researcher, a simple search could provide hundreds, if not thousands, of hits. In a lot of cases, some less than ethical individuals added to the confusion by including popular search terms in their Internet key search term areas. For example, a simple search for the word *Disney* might turn up numerous pornography sites.

Search engines were developed to avoid such sites. By 2000, searching had improved on the Web. At the same time, the average search would still lead to numerous unrelated hits. A number of search engine designers did a great deal of work to make sure that their site would deliver higher-quality searches.

At the same time, a lot of specialized sites began to spring up. A search for *complexity theory*, for example, will lead to a significant number of complexity-related sites. In a lot of cases, each site has links to numerous other sites that relate to complexity. In lot of cases, the extensive linking of related sites enables the researcher to quickly narrow the search to a number of high-quality sites. In the case of complexity theory, it would be possible to spend weeks analyzing all of the links that just 10 of the sites provide.

The Internet also creates a number of security problems for the average company. It is becoming increasingly apparent that hackers can successfully penetrate many of the corporate networks that are linked to the Web (most are linked as a matter of necessity). In a number of cases, hackers have penetrated government sites in the US, such as the Department of Defense.

The Internet (and computers) also makes information highly transferable. A disgruntled employee, or a hacker for that matter, can easily access sensitive corporate information and send it around the world in a matter of minutes. The existence of an Internet portal also means that the external espionage actor can be located anywhere in the world, as long as they are connected to the Web.

THE VIRTUAL WORKSPACE

The e-dimension also has a direct impact on the intelligence process. Companies have developed virtual workspaces in which analysts located around the world can share information, or even collaboratively work on research. The result is a diversity of input that is combined with exceptional speed. In one case, a company had its US team work on a project during the day in a virtual workspace that was then taken over by their European counterparts when they arrived at work. By using the virtual workspace, the time required for the project was substantially shortened. More importantly, the European counterparts were located in six different countries. That provided a unique country-specific aspect of the project that proved extremely valuable.

THE E-FUTURE IS NOW

The world really is not wired yet. Certainly, most people in the world have access to the Internet, but the technology infrastructure of 2001 will not compare with the technology infrastructure of, say, 2007. Those changes will certainly cause a frame-breaking shift in how and where intelligence is gathered and processed. There are a number of factors that will drive this radical change. Interestingly, each one by itself will not create the major shift. It is the convergence of these technologies that will drastically change everything.

The first of these developments is the movement toward a global wireless protocol. At the present time, someone traveling from the US to Europe must rent a phone for use in Europe. Most US systems are TDMA (time-division multiple access) or CDMA (code-division multiple access) – with one area of California using a variant of GSM (global system for mobile communications) – while most of Europe is using GSM. This simply means that phones from one country will not work in another country. There is movement toward the creation of phones that will work globally. No one knows just how this will be settled, but there is a lot of ongoing research in the area. In some cases, manufacturers are talking about dual-mode phones that will work with both protocols.

Another change is the new wireless broadband, or 3G (third generation) networks. The downturn in the technology market has delayed the deployment of these technologies, but as of 2001 Sprint PCS was conducting market testing of the networks in some areas. The

3G networks will support full-motion video transmission. This would mean that one person could talk to another on a television-quality connection.

There are also developments in the fiber-optic technologies of the world. New technologies that deploy light spectrum over the networks will multiply the capacity of the current networks.

The development of DSP (digital signal processing/processors) will also be a part of the change. DSPs are processors that can change an analogue signal into a digital signal. For example, an office voicemail could be converted to a text message by a DSP. The same is true of a fax. But it gets more interesting when softswitching is introduced to the mix. Softswitching is a new technology that will be deployed in the 2001–2002 time period. Softswitching allows an individual to remote-control the routing of all of their electronic devices. That includes paging, wireless, wired, etc. This is where the convergence effect comes in.

Within a few short months or years, the combination of a cellphone and a PDA (personal digital assistant) will drastically change how we communicate. For example, the deployment of DSP technology will enable faxes from home and the office to be digitized and converted into e-mail messages. Softswitching will allow the user to route all their paging, office and home voicemail, office and home faxes, and office and home e-mails to a single integrated PDA/cellphone combination. Add to that video capabilities, and the PDA/cellphone combination becomes a global communications device of unparalleled capability.

The implications are somewhat overwhelming. The intelligence analyst will be able to have access to high-speed data networks from almost anywhere in the world through the PDA/cellphone combination. With the added benefit of the new PDA portable keyboards – and the new computing capabilities of PDAs – the analyst can engage in the production of documents or have access to a global data resource no matter where they are located. The addition of interactive video capabilities at real-time speed and quality is a further benefit.

During the next five years, conventional computer-processing speeds are expected to exceed 4GHz. Within ten years, nanotechnology and optoelectronic applications are expected to create major increases in computer-processing speeds as well as data-storage capabilities.

The point of all of this is simple: the e-dimension is just beginning to impact the intelligence community. Within a few short years, the emergence of even more dynamic networks and integrated devices with unbelievable capabilities will again change much of the structure of intelligence processes. Along with all of that, the role of the intelligence professional will become still more important to the success of the organization.

NOTE

1 Ansoff, H.I. and McDonnell, E. (1990) *Implanting Strategic Management*, 2nd edn. Prentice Hall International (UK), Hertfordshire.

The Global Dimension

There is perhaps no other field that has so many global implications. This chapter discusses a number of the global issues that involve the intelligence community.

It is somewhat astounding that so few people, including those in the competitive intelligence area, actually understand the global dimension of the intelligence business. In spite of the continuing warnings from people like Michael Sekora, former head of the Reagan administration's Project Socrates, few heed such warnings. By its very nature, intelligence in the twenty-first century is driven by global players. Each of these competitors may have a drastically different set of ethical standards. The most important thing for the manager as well as the intelligence analyst to remember is that most, if not all, of these global competitors are working in your country.

It was 1993 and a major news organization expressed an interest in doing a story about the global intelligence community. They had asked Pat Chaote (a former candidate for vice-president of the US and an expert in global competition) and myself to appear. They also had one request: "We need an executive from one of these companies to be willing to appear with you and tell their story. We want them to be willing to explain how a foreign intelligence operative was able to penetrate their security and take an important technology secret."

It was a great story and a great opportunity for some of these executives to get the true story out. There was just one problem. None were willing to go on record and discuss their daily battle with foreign intelligence activities. It quickly became abundantly clear that they feared reprisal. It also became clear that, in some cases, they feared for their personal safety. Thus, the story went no further.

This simple story illustrates a few of the challenges that companies face in dealing with the global nature of intelligence. There is no shared ethical standard between different groups. There are some in the global community who would think nothing of going past the line of simple intimidation. That is the reality. The key is to understand the nature of the global competitive forces, and to develop effective strategies for dealing with them.

THE THIN LINE BETWEEN INTELLIGENCE AND COUNTER-INTELLIGENCE

When President Clinton went to Japan to discuss the imbalance of trade with that country, he returned victorious, or so he declared. In his discussions with the Japanese, he asked for voluntary restrictions on the part of the Japanese in the export of automobiles to the US. In their discussions, the Japanese agreed to discuss the matter further. Clinton responded by announcing victory.

Those who understand Japanese culture will appreciate that they said "no" to Clinton. For anyone who has studied Japanese culture, it follows that the failure to say "yes" means that the answer is "no." That is their culture. The failure to understand the culture of another country has caused many problems for business people. In the case of the Japanese, they make sure that they understand the culture of another country extremely well before they go there.

A number of years ago, a an individual named Louis Leclerc at Monash University in Australia wrote an extremely insightful paper on this topic titled "Does America say yes to Japan?"[1] The author apparently married a Japanese woman and moved to Japan for a time. What he discovered was a country that was actively engaged in an economic war. He witnessed a level of co-operation between government and business that does not exist in any other country. He also found that the original language article "A Japan that can say no" by Akio Morita, the head of Sony at the time, revealed many of the true attitudes and strategies of Japan as a country. Further, the truth was quite different from the public façade that is presented to the world. The thrust of the article is that Japan is still at war (economically) and almost any actions can be justified to win that war.

Understanding the Japanese model

Today's Japanese culture is founded in its history. Centuries ago, a culture that was based on what is called the *Han* system developed in Japan. Each region of the country had a ruler called a *daimyo*. The warriors or *samurai* supported the daimyo. The daimyo had absolute power over the common people, including the right to take any life that he wanted to. Over the years, this system of control became a part of the culture. That is, rather than resenting the level of control exercised by the daimyo, the people began to embrace it as their way of life.

The consolidation of power in the hands of an emperor did not change the system. The people still valued total compliance. In the 1800s, a number of events eroded some aspects of the Japanese system. The major change was an end to the isolationism of the country, in favor of becoming a participant in the global economy. At the same time, the Han-type culture remained.

Large trading companies called *zaibatsu* were formed. At the end of World War II, the occupying forces told the Japanese that the zaibatsu were actually trusts, and they were made illegal. Of course that was no problem for the Japanese: they just changed the name of the zaibatsu to *keiretsu*. The result today is the seven keiretsu that are such familiar names to global consumers.

During the war, one ministry had distinguished itself among all other aspects of the Japanese war machine. That was the Ministry of Munitions. With the end of the war, the ministry was of course disbanded, but the unit itself remained intact. The new name was the Ministry of International Trade and Industry (MITI). The transition was so seamless that the new organization employed the same people, the same office space, even the same telephones as its predecessor agency. As a quasi-government/business entity, the new MITI became a country co-ordinator for intelligence and business co-ordination.

Understanding the historic roots of present-day Japan helps intelligence (and counter-intelligence) personnel understand their competitors. Add to that a culture in which deception, or even theft, is acceptable and the competitor becomes formidable. But there is more. A number of countries have adopted a Japanese-style approach to intelligence. That includes the French and certainly the mainland Chinese, among others. The French have also adopted much of the Japanese strategy involving the protection of home markets.

An interesting organization is the Japan External Trade Organization (JETRO). It was formed in the early 1990s with the stated purpose of helping American companies do business in Japan. Experience has revealed that there are other purposes behind the organization. There have been persistent rumors that JETRO is viewed by certain US government agencies as one of the most sophisticated intelligence-gathering organizations working in the US.[2] Over the last decade, numerous examples have been cited in which a Japanese company gets involved with an American company and ends up controlling the firm in short order.

An excellent book on the topic is John J. Fialka's *War by Other Means: Economic espionage in America*.[3] One of the things he points out is the extent of the targeting of US and Canadian firms for espionage. He also suggests that most visitors to Japanese hotels, for example, do not understand that the telephones are basically "always on." That is, they are bugging devices, so that every conversation a visiting business person might have is recorded.

A number of years ago, Michael Sekora of Technology Strategic Planning, Inc., visited a major US manufacturer. He had done his homework prior to the visit, and had discovered that the firm's entire product development process had been compromised. Here is how it had been accomplished (Fig. 5.1). Each supplier had American management and was an old-line strategic partner of the US company. What Sekora discovered, however, was that through a complex set of organizational ownership situations, all of the companies had been secretly acquired by the US firm's major international competitor.

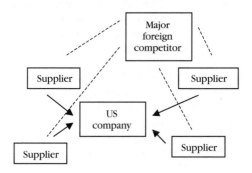

Fig. 5.1 The Japanese system of company–supplier partnership makes this US company vulnerable to infiltration by a foreign competitor.

At that point in time, the US company was using (what else?) the Japanese system of partnering with suppliers. As a result, the company had shared almost all of its product development plans for the next five years. All, the company thought, were well-kept secrets. Astoundingly, the US firm would not believe Sekora's information. Sekora determined that through the strategic partnering arrangement that the firm had with its suppliers, the Japanese competitor had acquired virtually all of the product plans the company had for the next five years.

LEARNING BEST PRACTICE: KODAK

Companies that compete well in the global environment understand the need to develop extensive intelligence information about the countries and cultures into which they will go. One lesson learned by an American company in Japan a few years ago illustrates this fact quite well.

As a way of opening the door in the Japanese market, the American company Kodak decided to throw a party and invite all of the key executives and staff of the six major keiretsu in the country. These keiretsu control almost all of the business in the Japanese economy and are closely linked with the Japanese government as well.

To make sure their Japanese guests appreciated them, Kodak made sure that ample supplies of a Japanese beer were available to their guests. Upon arriving and seeing the beer, the guests from every company but one immediately turned and walked out. Shocked, the American executives frantically tried to find out what was wrong.

They discovered that every keiretsu owns one company in every industry, including a beer company. The beer that a company serves is an indication of which keiretsu a company is affiliated with. In Japan, that means that the other keiretsu will not do business with a keiretsu competitor's company. By serving the beer of only one keiretsu, the managers of Kodak had sent the message that they were controlled by, and affiliated with, one individual keiretsu.

The best companies go to great lengths to gather information about the customs and norms of target market countries. In the case of American Airlines, when they were granted the rights to fly to Japan, they conducted extensive research about all aspects of Japanese culture, customs, food, and so on. As a result, American was able to inaugurate service with the full support of the Japanese government and people.

The companies that do this well also understand the role of such intelligence in the larger area of competitive intelligence. The case study of Motorola Japan in Chapter 7 is a good illustration of how intelligence-gathering about culture and customs enabled a firm to obtain some very necessary technology intelligence.

GLOBALIZATION AND COMPETITION

One of the benefits (and curses) of working in law enforcement is that it takes little time for an individual to reach a point at which they trust no one. From a law enforcement standpoint, this attitude helps protect the police officer. It means that they maintain an awareness (and innate distrust) of everyone and everything around them. Nothing is ever assumed.

That same principle is important for any firm doing business in today's global environment. The cleaning crew at a firm's office building often experiences very high employee turnover. Often, little is done to check references on workers who apply with office-cleaning companies. Someone intent on penetrating a firm's security has to do little more than apply for a job with their office-cleaning company. In short order, the office can be wired for video and sound, phones can be tapped, and all faxes can be acquired. In most cases, this can be done in less than a week.

Another threat to a firm's security is from its own employees. It is little challenge for a competitor's intelligence representative to make contact with a firm's employees. Those with financial difficulties, drug or alcohol problems, or grudges against the company make prime targets for those who want to obtain company secrets. Additionally, few companies have arrangements to protect themselves from internal staff. Laws in countries like the US may prohibit appropriate research into an individual's background to determine if they might have a predisposition toward stealing company information.

THE ULTIMATE PROBLEM: DENIAL

Most managers, especially in the US, have problems believing that competitors might engage in unethical or illegal intelligence-gathering activities. Even those that do will often not believe that their information has been compromised. In the event that there is a theft, managers are often shocked to discover that it was their most trusted employee who participated in the act.

Benchmarking has historically been little more than the copying and improving of competitors' products. In the new global economy, there are competitors who do not share the ethical standards of the Society of Competitive Intelligence Professionals. Many find it hard to believe that for some competitors, prostitution, threats, or even murder may be justifiable in the acquisition of a competitor's intellectual property.

Companies competing in the new global economy must develop a new mental toughness if they are to protect their trade secrets. Here are a few keys to accomplishing this objective.

1 Trust no one. Always design systems that ensure the protection of critical or sensitive information.
2 Conduct background checks on all individuals who might have periodic access to the company premises.
3 Supervise maintenance and repair personnel while they are on company premises.
4 Proactively plan for attempted intrusions of office space, computer systems, and communications equipment.
5 Segregate sensitive information in secure work areas. Control access to those areas.
6 Employ a full-time security expert to protect company information.
7 Periodically hire an external security consultant to review all security issues.

Few people realize that many of the innovations that companies bring to market were first stolen from a competitor. Ethical behavior is extremely important; at the same time, protecting a company from espionage is equally important. This is the reality of the new global economy. In a lot of cases, there are competitors who will use every technology tool available, and will stop at nothing to acquire a company's intellectual capital. This is the new intelligence reality of the twenty-first century.

NOTES

1 Leclerc, L. "Does America say yes to Japan?" Available online at ftp.monash.edu.au in the directory /pub/nihongo as a zip file.

2 Holstein, W.J. (2001) "With friends like these." *US News and World Report*, July 22.

3 Fialka, J.J. (1997) *War by Other Means: Economic espionage in America*. Norton, London and New York. For an excellent excerpt, go to www.nytimes.com/books/first/f/fialka-war.html

The State of the Art

Technological changes, plus the introduction of a number of new processes, have had a significant impact on the field of intelligence. This chapter discusses these issues, as well as considering a systematic process for conducting effective intelligence.

To some extent, the field of intelligence has been immune to much of the debate that has recently been going on in the fields of management and strategy. The conflict between linear and non-linear mental models has come to the fore in these fields. On the one hand, the equilibrium theory (linear) thinkers contend that historic competencies, SWOT analysis, Five Forces analysis, and competitive advantage are still viable constructs from which to plan and manage. On the other, the complex adaptive systems (non-linear) thinkers suggest that such tools are no longer of value. Most of the intelligence community is still tied to the linear mental models.

As a result, there has been stagnation in some segments of the intelligence area. At the same time, a number of leading-edge intelligence thinkers have wisely adapted a number of powerful tools to the practice of intelligence. What is needed is a systems approach to the field of intelligence. Equilibrium-based (linear) mental models of management and strategy thinking are still the norm at almost all global companies. As complex systems theory applications grow, it is suggested that company leadership teams will begin to understand the long-term value of organizational learning and the critical role that intelligence must play in it.

COMPETITIVE INTELLIGENCE TODAY

Although intelligence professionals in many organizations feel disconnected or segregated from their organization's strategy process, this is not how it should be. In looking at an organization as a complex adaptive system operating in a complex dynamic environment (see *Complexity and Paradox*[1] in this series for more information on this topic), the profit-critical link between organizational learning (and thus intelligence) and strategy development is clear. At the same time, the intelligence community continues to be tied to equilibrium-based mental models that assume linearity instead of complexity.

There is abundant information that relates mental models and managers' abilities to create effective organizational strategy for complex environments. This means the assessment models deployed by the intelligence analyst have a great deal to do with the quality of the output. To put it another way, a simplistic model will lack effectiveness if the environment is expected to be one of rapid change and high levels of complexity.

TRADITIONAL TOOLS

The classification of intelligence sources began in the military/intelligence community with the following basic definitions.

» *HUMINT (human intelligence)* – information derived from a person or persons possessing either first- or second-hand information about an area of interest.
» *SIGINT (signal intelligence)* – information derived from electronic intelligence.
» *IMINT (imagery intelligence)* – information derived from some type of imagery, such as photographs.

All of these intelligence sources continue to be used in the business intelligence community. In some cases, they are used illegally or unethically.

Another carry-over from the military/intelligence community is source and information evaluation. These applications are still valuable today.

» *Source evaluation* – a method of evaluating and classifying the level of reliability or confidence that the analyst places in the source itself.
  » A = a source that is always reliable.
  » B = a source that is usually reliable.
  » C = a source that is sometimes reliable.
  » D = a source that is usually unreliable.
  » E = a source that is of unknown reliability.
» *Information evaluation* – a method of analyzing and classifying the reliability or trustworthiness of the information itself.
  » 1 = information that is most certainly accurate and true.
  » 2 = information that is probably true.
  » 3 = information that may or may not be true.
  » 4 = information that is probably untrue.
  » 5 = information that is clearly untrue.

The two systems are then combined to give an intelligence team a common language for use in qualifying the level of confidence the analyst has in both the source and the information. For example, an A-1 classification would mean that the source is highly dependable and that the information derived from the source is most likely accurate and true. An A-3 classification might mean that the source, even though highly reliable, indicated that the information was questionable or that the analyst had reason to question the reliability of the information.

Those in the intelligence community use a similar system, whether or not it is explicitly defined. For example, in conducting Delphi panels or modified Delphi panels (see below), a good analyst should be able to rank the reliability of the experts. Often, when conducting expert research and interviews of this type, it is not unusual to find a supposed expert who is 10 or more years out of date in their knowledge base. Good analysts are smart enough to eliminate these sources and work with ones that are more reliable.

The same is true of the information itself. *Dissonant data* – information that is some degree out of agreement with the consensus – needs to be investigated. It is not unusual to find that the source with the dissonant data is the one that is most accurate and that all of the other sources are lacking in contemporary content.

It is not unusual for a team of researchers to reject an eyewitness account in favor of the opinions of accepted "experts" in a field. Such was the case in the 1960s when a group of senior consultants would not believe their junior analyst's report on Japanese steel mill technology deployments because a group of respected "experts" had told them that the technology would not be deployed by the Japanese for another 20 years. (Which confirms the validity of the often-heard comment in law enforcement: "Who are you going to believe, me or your lying eyes?")

The military/intelligence establishment (like the research establishment) helped establish the practice of formulating hypotheses for intelligence-gathering and analysis. In formulating a hypothesis, a number of propositions are developed. They might be the results that the researcher expects to find. The researcher then uses the information-gathering process to either prove or disprove the propositions, or hypothesis. Bias is a problem for any researcher, so the idea of converting an intelligence "need" into various hypotheses is an excellent starting point for any project. In using hypotheses, the researcher categorizes information related to whether or not it supports the various hypotheses that were formulated. In this way, the researcher should be forced to deal with their biases or blind spots.

TECHNOLOGY TOOLS

In the 1980s, a number of databases were converted to computer-based search files. By the early 1990s, a significant number of databases were available for computer searches. As the Internet exploded in the 1990s, a number of these became accessible over the Internet. By 2001, the World Wide Web had become the equivalent of a worldwide library. In just over 20 years, the manner and method of accessing information has changed radically.

The World Wide Web changed other aspects of intelligence. By the twenty-first century, information was travelling the world in seconds rather than the days or weeks it had taken before. The ability to transfer large files of information electronically – on the Internet – also changed the intelligence industry.

By 2001, a company called STRATFOR (otherwise known as Strategic Forecasting) had completely changed the intelligence process again. With over 100,000 worldwide subscribers to its daily intelligence report,[2] STRATFOR had developed a global intelligence network resource that was faster and, in many cases, better than many of the best government intelligence services could provide. In fact, many of STRATFOR's clients were these very services.

TOOLS WITH MARGINAL VALUE

With the emergence of complexity-based thinking, a number of the traditional tools that have been historically used in intelligence are coming into question. Three come to mind.

The first is SWOT (strengths, weaknesses, opportunities, and threats) analysis. Most intelligence consulting firms, as well as corporate intelligence units, still use this tool. Some might suggest it is still a good starting point in an analysis. From a mental model standpoint, the approach is questionable. A company's strengths, weaknesses, opportunities, and threats may have some value in assessing the current state of an entity. What is missing in such an analysis is the reality of the environment. The new nature of the environment as a complex dynamic system means that what a company or a competitor does well may become irrelevant over very short intervals of time. In other words, the use of a linear or static profile of a company is somewhat useless in light of the reality of a rapidly changing, complex environment.

Another tool of deteriorating value is the Five Forces model. This tool was popularized in Michael Porter's book *Competitive Advantage*.[3] Basically, Porter hypothesized that it was possible to understand an industry by evaluating five key forces (Fig. 6.1). Empirical research does not provide a great deal of support for the Five Forces model.[4] Generally, the model is popular because it is somewhat simple in nature. Ansoff suggests that it fails to meet the demands of the complex reality of the environment because it leads to what he calls "strategic generalities" that are "difficult to apply in practice."[5] In the introduction to his book *Hypercompetition*, Richard D'Aveni suggests that the equilibrium-based theories "all fall apart when the dynamics of competition are considered."[6]

Fig. 6.1 The Five Forces Model.

Further, since the hypothesis is based upon equilibrium theory (linear), the complex adaptive systems theorists would not support it.

In reality, the forces that affect a business are significantly more complex and dynamic than those presented in the Five Forces model. Even the Ten Forces model developed by this writer has the same deficiency.[7] Simply put, complex environments require complex analysis.

A third tool that is widely used in the intelligence community is benchmarking. Gary Hamel and C.K. Prahalad, among others, have concluded that benchmarking can be problematic at best. In environments of rapid change, benchmarking does little more that reveal what a competitor used to do. Leading-edge competitors are in a constant state of change. That is, they are continually changing.

Even the Japanese, who really invented the idea of benchmarking, do not use it in the same manner as many US intelligence firms use it. "Best practice" is nothing more than something that someone did at some point in time that worked. This does not mean that it will work for your organization in meeting the demands of the current environment at this point in time. Simply put, benchmarking is not an effective tool for complex environments.

NEW APPLICATIONS

A number of techniques have been developed to deal with the uncertainty of decision-making in the new environment of the twenty-first century. One such technique is the Delphi technique. In using a *Delphi technique* or *Delphi panel*, the researcher develops a set of questions that offer an exhaustive range of responses. For example, the responses may range from "very low" to "very high" and offer two or three responses that fall between the two extremes. The questions are then posed to a group of six or more experts. The researcher will revisit the respondents until all are at a general level of agreement.

This is a cumbersome and sometimes difficult process. As a result, I have used what I call a *modified Delphi panel* on a number of projects. It is important to remember that Delphi panels can be quite predictive when it comes to issues that have a high level of unpredictability. That is what makes them so valuable for organizations facing complex, or high unpredictable, futures.

A modified Delphi simply involves a source evaluation. Rather than using six experts, the researcher will use eight to ten experts. In posing the questions to the experts, it quickly becomes apparent which ones really understand the topic under study and which ones do not. In using a modified Delphi, the less-than-qualified experts are eliminated and only those that appear to understand the problem are considered.

This approach has proven extremely accurate in predicting future environments.

SPEED

High levels of complexity and rates of change characterize the new competitive environment of the twenty-first century. As a result, what used to work well may not be appropriate any longer. There are a number of ways to deal with these issues.

First, technology can substantially increase the speed at which information can be gathered. In 1997, I beta-tested an Internet-based expert panel approach that was designed to involve multiple feedback sessions over a short period of time. The test provided very good results.

Another similar use of the Internet is the use of on-call expert panels. The experts are organized around areas of expertise. If the firm needs rapid information of extremely high quality, the experts are polled via email. This method can work extremely well as long as the appropriate remuneration is available. If well organized, the process can provide extremely good information about a topic in 48–72 hours.

In the case of STRATFOR, the number of respondents they have around the world makes their information extremely good. In a number of areas of conflict, STRATFOR has provided the most accurate information available from any source. As technology diffuses throughout more parts of the world, STRATFOR's network will just get better.

SCENARIOS

The use of scenarios in the intelligence community has been growing in popularity over the past 10 or so years. There are a number of reasons for this. First, since scenarios are non-linear in nature, they are especially well suited for environments of low predictability. Scenarios fit the intelligence processes quite well also. The use of extensive intelligence gathering to begin analyzing the driving forces related to the topic is a good basis for developing scenarios. Good intelligence, plus things like CEO attribute profiling, can enhance the accuracy of the scenarios. Both scenarios and war-gaming can be quite beneficial in overcoming resistance to change within the organization.

WAR-GAMING

War-gaming has become extremely popular over the last few years. Again, this is due to the highly unpredictable nature of the global environment. War-gaming is another process that has been borrowed from the military establishment. It can be quite effective in getting people to think "outside the box," which is extremely important for maintaining competitiveness in highly turbulent environments.

A few years ago, an associate and I were asked to plan and facilitate a seminar on war-gaming. I had been doing research about the convergence of computer and telephony technologies. We concluded that the best way to teach war-gaming was to involve the group in an actual war-gaming experience. So after a short introductory session, the group was divided into small groups, with each one being told to assume the role of the executive team of a major computer and telephony company.

The teams competed by discussing their strategy for a period of time (timed periods are important in this process), and then presenting their new strategy to the entire group. The first round went as expected, but the second round produced a definite change in how each team was thinking. They began to think more proactively.

All of the groups had been given a packet with a strategic profile of all of the companies (similar to the Apple Computer profile shown in Chapter 7). In some cases, the teams set about correcting their gaps or deficiencies as part of their strategy – a very good move. When the groups got to the third pass, it became apparent that all of them were becoming much more aggressive. I observed a few "messengers" quietly passing between different groups.

As each group got up to present their new strategy at the end of the third pass, it became obvious that one computer company, one software company, and one telephony manufacturer were very quietly holding back so that they could be the last to present. When the time came for one of the three to present, all three went to the front of the room. They announced that they had agreed to merge, which would result in the creation of one of the most dynamic integrated technology companies in the world.

The scenario took less than three hours. Had it occurred as a facilitated war game for a real company, the developments that took place in the short time period would have been somewhat shocking to the firm's management. At the same time, the exercise would have forced the management team to look at a situation that they had not previously considered.

AN INTELLIGENCE PROCESS THAT WORKS

Any time intelligence-gathering, processing, and dissemination of analysis is involved, resistance to change is also involved. Seasoned intelligence professionals know that managing the flow and acceptance of information is just as important as gathering and analyzing it.

Well-executed intelligence projects tend to have a predictable flow to them. In looking at such projects (both successful and not so successful), it becomes apparent that the manager of the intelligence function must deal with a number of issues in order to ensure success. Figure 6.2 represents a process that deals with these issues.

The intelligence process involves numerous challenges. At the beginning of the process, the researcher has to have access to some critically important information. That involves understanding three issues:

1 turnaround time required for the project;
2 the urgency of the project; and
3 the impact or importance of the project.

In some cases, senior managers may not feel comfortable in sharing all of the required information. There are two responses to such feelings. First, those in the intelligence group should have been rigorously investigated during the selection process. Their integrity and ability to keep information confidential should not be a question. Second, if an individual in the intelligence group cannot be trusted, they should be removed. Either way, the intelligence team must have the information that they need to meet the needs of the firm effectively, or there is little point in going forward.

Next, the researcher needs to understand the specific needs that require to be met in the project. There is often a difference between

Process activities/input   The intelligence process

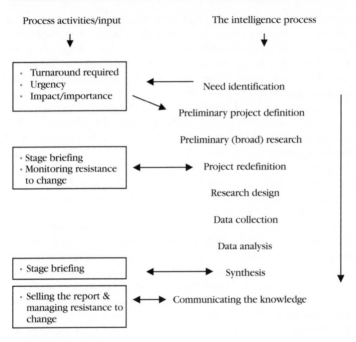

Fig. 6.2 The intelligence process, as used by managers of successful intelligence projects.

how the project is described and the actual need that is supposed to be met. Early efforts by the researcher to understand the needs underlying the project can reap rewards at the end of the project.

Another thing the researcher needs to arrange early in the process is periodic briefings, or *stage briefings*. There are two reasons for conducting stage briefings. First, preliminary research often leads to other issues. The researcher needs client direction about those issues. Second and most importantly, stage briefings are actually there for the purpose of managing resistance to change. If the client team is periodically briefed as a project progresses, a systematic "adoption" of the new or dissonant information will begin to occur. Most intelligence findings are not rejected because they are poorly done. They are rejected because the information contained in the research is different from the mental model of the client. The periodic briefings are quite helpful in breaking down the barrier of paradigm blindness.

Once the needs are identified and the preliminary project definition is complete, the researcher will normally conduct broad research. That is, they will attempt to obtain a broad overview of the information on the topic. Normally, the researcher will formulate hypotheses at this point in the project or, in some cases, they may formulate them at the very beginning of the project. Either way, by the end of the broad research exercise, the researcher will begin challenging the hypotheses with the information that has been gathered.

At this point a stage briefing with the client can be extremely helpful. Getting the client's hypotheses can also be helpful if that is possible. If the project needs adjustment or change, it is done at this point. In some cases, for example, the broad research may reveal that more expensive fieldwork is necessary, or that expert panels will need to be used.

Before completing the final research design and going forward, any areas of concern should be resolved. The researcher needs to be confident that the desired information will be obtained from the research. Again, it is important to remember that no two projects are identical. Ensuring that the final research design meets the client's needs is important.

Most of the time, early results begin leading the researcher to certain conclusions. In one technology shift study, which involved questionnaires that were completed by customers, it became immediately clear that the research team and the client had totally missed the point in their assumptions. After looking at the first 10 questionnaires, the team knew exactly where the study was going to go.

This study involved the shift from a mechanically-based application to an electronically-based application. The team and the client believed that it would be seven to ten years before the shift would occur. The study revealed that the demand would shift in a matter of 36 months. The good news: the client already had the electronically-based solution. All they had to do was step up their implementation plans.

REAL-WORLD APPLICATION

In 1996, my team was retained to investigate the future of switching technologies for an international telecommunications equipment manufacturer. At the outset, it seemed like a fairly simple and straightforward project. The broad preliminary research seemed to confirm our suspicions that there would be no frame-breaking technology shifts over the next five to seven years.

One day my researcher came in and told me that she had been running into some information that ran contrary to the general flow of information. It had popped up on just a few searches, but it did concern her. As we studied it together, we began to ask ourselves about the impact of the alternative technology if it ever became a reality. It would have been substantial.

She proceeded to expand her search for more information on the topic. Finally, she discovered that a well-respected (and very expensive) organization had done a paper on the topic. I decided to call the client to brief him on our progress and to see if he had any idea about how we could get access to the research.

The client listened quietly, and seemed to be interested in the fact that we were having doubts about some of the assumptions that many of the supposed experts were making about the slow shift in technology. I then asked him if he had heard of the report we were interested in getting. "I have a copy," he replied. "I'll send you a copy overnight."

A little stunned, I politely asked him why he had not given us the report along with the other research that he had provided when he gave us the project. "I wanted to see if you were good enough to find the information. Your suspicions are confirming some of the same suspicions that we have had."

As a result, we modified our research design, and expanded our investigation into the other technology area. Ultimately, we found and interviewed the top expert in the field, who had been involved in much of the research. As it turned out, the major technology shift was going to occur.

There were a couple of lessons learned on that project. First, since it was our first project for this client, he wanted to test us to see if we would dig until we found the information. By going back for a stage briefing, we were able to reorient the project once our suspicions were confirmed. Second, we learned that if something seems out of the ordinary, no matter how small the item might be, the intuitive researcher will follow the trail until the answer is found.

EMERGING CHANGES IN INTELLIGENCE

The field of intelligence is undergoing change. On the one hand, many aspects are not changing. On the other, there is radical change. Not only has technology changed how the researcher can gather intelligence, but it has also drastically changed the speed at which information can be gathered.

Industrial or economic espionage has changed too. The former military and governmental intelligence personnel of some countries are now plying their trade in acquiring trade secrets. New technologies, such as the wireless 3G networks that are to be unveiled in late 2001 and early 2002, will make it possible for an intelligence operative to wire a competitor's research laboratory and executive offices. Once wired, it will be possible to send full motion video and sound to their office and ultimately to their home country.

As a result of heightened levels of complexity and faster rates of change, intelligence practitioners are adopting new approaches in gathering and analyzing information. Further, they are developing new ways of managing resistance to change in presenting their findings.

The intelligence industry is certainly changing. Further, the importance of the intelligence function at organizations is becoming increasingly important, and even appreciated at some companies.

NOTES

1 Underwood, J.D. (2002) *Complexity and Paradox*. Capstone, Oxford.
2 Available online at www.stratfor.com
3 Porter, M.E. (1985) *Competitive Advantage*. The Free Press, New York.
4 Ghemawat, P. (2000) *Strategy and the Business Landscape*. Prentice Hall, Upper Saddle River, NJ.

5 Ansoff, H.I. (1990) "A strategic success paradigm for the 21st century." *Unpublished article*, San Diego, CA.

6 D'Aveni, R. (1994) *Hypercompetition*. The Free Press, New York.

7 Underwood, J.D. (2001) *Thriving in E-Chaos*. Prima Publishers, Roseville, CA.

In Practice

This chapter features four case studies of real intelligence projects.

In a practical sense, there is no one great illustration of an excellent intelligence case. The reason is, by the very nature of the beast, that each project has different challenges and different demands. There are issues of time, urgency, internal politics, and competitor misinformation that must be dealt with, as well as the position of the individual bringing the need.

The quality of an intelligence project has more to do with the person conducting the research and analysis than anything else. Some people function simply as data collectors and think that is intelligence. Still others seem to generate artful, insightful analysis of similar situations. As one friend in the intelligence business suggested, there are two reasons that some people are exceptional in conducting intelligence research. First, some people are simply gifted. They just have an exceptional ability to do the work. Second, they are persistent. As one individual said, "exceptional intelligence is 1% inspiration and 99% perspiration."

CASE STUDY 1: SBC COMMUNICATIONS/SOUTHWESTERN BELL

The competitive challenges of deregulation

The following case study was submitted by John McMaster, former director of competitive intelligence at the US firm SBC Communications from 1995 to 2000. John is now an independent consultant who provides intelligence information to corporate clients.

In the late 1980s, small companies then called competitive access providers (CAPs) began offering large businesses high-speed access and data services on a local basis, similar to the way that MCI started competing with AT&T for long distance. Primarily connecting a large business to their long-distance carriers or interexchange carriers (IXCs), these CAPs were competing with the incumbent local exchange carrier (ILEC), and in most cases a regional Bell operating company (RBOC). Many of these CAPs had "deep pockets" and were well funded, in part, by the major IXCs (AT&T, MCI, and Sprint) wanting to decrease their costs and reliance on the RBOCs, as well as capture part of the $100bn local telecommunications market.

Southwestern Bell was once the smallest of the RBOCs and is now an operating company of SBC Communications after acquiring

Pacific Telesis, Ameritech, and Southern New England Telephone. Southwestern Bell recognized the threat to its revenues from CAPs and formed a competitive intelligence operation in 1989. Over the next several years, technology advances such as, fiber networking, digital switching, and the development of the Internet enabled CAPs to expand their service offerings into switched services and the local exchange market. Hence, their name changed from CAPs to competitive local exchange carriers (CLECs). Meanwhile, Southwestern Bell and the other RBOCs were seeing their local revenues diminish with competition and began lobbying for regulatory reforms that would enable them to expand their revenues by entering the long-distance market.

Southwestern Bell had to find a way to protect and grow its revenues, while showing that it had competition in order to get the regulatory reforms it needed to enter the long-distance market. Its competitive intelligence unit was tasked with supporting both these initiatives. The unit had already collected a lot of information on the locations where CLECs were operating, what their fiber networks looked like, and how customers were being targeted, but verifying this information and putting it into a form that lobbyists could use with regulators and lawmakers to show what was at risk was more difficult.

A process was developed that later became known as the competitive risk analysis. One of the critical inputs to the process was documenting and digitizing competitive fiber routes. This was derived from CLEC sales collateral, outside plant technician sightings, reports from sales representatives, and other secondary information such as press releases and regulatory filings. Physical verification of the fiber routes was done by actually driving the routes and documenting the locations on a map. This information was then put into a mapping program to digitize it. CLEC switch and collocation information was also included. In addition, business customer locations were geocoded (latitude and longitude co-ordinate association) and information on the types of customers CLECs were targeting was used to sharpen the analysis (number of business lines and revenue per business). Risk factors were then associated with each business customer in the top 10 metropolitan area within South-western Bell's territory. These risk factors for each customer included:

1 the proximity to fiber;
2 the billed revenue;

3 the number of business lines;
4 the number of CLECs operating in the serving wire center area; and
5 the presence of an interconnection and collocation agreements in a
   serving wire center.

Values were associated with each risk factor and summed up to classify each customer as high, medium, or low risk.

Ultimately, the analysis indicated that while only 7% of the business customers could be considered as a high risk to competition, CLECs were targeting these customers and could capture over 30% of the business revenues in the top 10 major metropolitan areas. To illustrate and package this intelligence, the competitive intelligence unit used mapping software to overlay high- and medium-risk customers onto serving wire center areas and competitive fiber. The result was a competitive analysis used by lobbyists to pass the Telecommunications Act of 1996. Former FCC chairman, Peter Huber, said: "This is the best study I've seen from an RBOC." Internally, the study was used to target areas for further network development and to pinpoint high-risk customers for sales and marketing efforts. Some additional value from the study was derived by adding a competitive risk marker on business customer records to help sales representatives protect an estimated $37mn in annual revenues.

In late 1995, a similar analysis was developed to assess the potential of cable telephony and broadband competition. The competitive intelligence unit, in conjunction with tips from sales representatives and outside plant technicians, identified the network components of cable TV companies being deployed and the extent of deployment. The components consisted of fiber networks, repeaters, and fiber nodes that could be used to provide two-way cable services and cable modems. Actual field surveys were used to verify reports and document cable TV network deployment. The documentation was then packaged with other facts and pictures illustrating cable TV activity in the major metropolitan areas. Using mapping software, the cable TV components were overlaid onto maps that enabled clients to see the extent and capability of potential competition from cable TV companies. In addition, the types and locations of customers that could be targeted were also identified. Updated for several years, results from these studies were used in SBC's $6bn broadband deployment decision and investment. One can only imagine why the initiative was named Project Pronto. Nevertheless, SBC Communications has emerged as the largest provider of broadband DSL (digital subscriber line) services. Only time will tell if the investment was made soon enough to overcome cable TV's broadband services.

> ### KEY LESSONS
>
> » Intelligence is more about perspiration than it is about inspiration. Often, the intelligence solution is provided by hard work and determination on the part of the analyst.
> » There is no substitute for HUMINT (human intelligence).

CASE STUDY 2: THE AUTHOR AS GRADUATE

A personal journey

One of my first forays into the intelligence business was as a graduate student in the 1970s. At the time, the students on the team had little or no understanding of the magnitude of their research, but we did get a sense that the project was a lot bigger than we were led to believe it was.

Every graduate student in our program dreaded the research course taught by Dr Jim Makens. He was the only professor who taught the course, and he had a reputation for expecting exceptional work. Student-level work was unacceptable in his class: he expected the work turned out by his graduate students to be on a par with that of the major consulting firms. Under Dr Makens's leadership, the university began doing research for a number of major international companies. In the case of my team, we were assigned to a global technology company that had roots in the defense arena as well as geophysical services.

Dr Makens was none too shy about making sure that his students represented the university well. In one situation, a student team was presenting their research findings to the CEO and senior staff of a large company. At some point in the proceedings, Makens realized that the research was flawed. At that point he apologized to the executives and advised the students that they had just flunked the class.

Our first introduction to our client involved a lot of security issues. After going through a lot of different steps in gaining admittance to the client's facility, we were led down a corridor that contained doors with special security locks on them. This puzzled the team a bit, since we were to meet with the geophysical group of the firm. Finally we were led into a meeting room to meet our client, a geologist.

The client explained that his firm was doing a study of the oil fields of the world, and needed information about one specific area of the world: the USSR. We were a little puzzled by all of this, since we assumed that there must already be a lot of information out there. The client was especially interested in the locations of major oil fields, the formation the fields were in, and the depth of the producing fields.

The early research on the project seemed to go quite well. The team began searching all available publications and developing a list of experts that could be interviewed. About four weeks into the project, a troublesome pattern emerged. It seems that the Russians were quite open in revealing the information that we were looking for. Major publications, in conducting a world oil survey each year, would get the location, formation, reserves, and depth of formation from around the world, including Russia. That's where the project became a challenge.

The team member responsible for compiling the data informed the team that he had discovered a problem. It seems that the Russians were playing games with their information. One year they would disclose one set of data for the oil reserves of the USSR. The next year, they would "flip" the data, listing the reserve information for one field as the information for an entirely different field. This had been going on for years. (Maybe that's why our client was willing to give some struggling graduate students the opportunity to attempt the project.)

Obviously, panic set in. The team had visions of being publicly humiliated over our failure to get the client's information. The more we dug, the more we found that the information had been masterfully confused. As with a lot of intelligence projects, the team was back at the beginning again.

Further research led the team to a few Russian geologists, of whom two or three were living in the US. The team actually located two of the experts. Both were quite old, and were unable to help. In a few cases, a number of Russian geologists that had defected to the US were located.

The team was able to get a little information from them, but generally they each confirmed the problem we had already discovered. Even the defectors had been given limited access to the data we needed.

By this time, the team was in a total panic. We had found defectors, even a Russian geologist who had discovered one of the major fields, but he was simply too old to be able to visit with us. As the end of the semester approached, and the time for the client presentation loomed near, the team redoubled its efforts. Still, no breakthrough.

Then one of the team members began calling all of the associations that were involved in the oil industry. Often, associations will maintain a corporate library for members, so the team decided to see if there was any area they had overlooked.

The call to the American Petroleum Association was answered by a pleasant voice. After listening to our problem, the lady on the phone said she remembered that one of their experts might have done some work in that area. "Could I take your number and ask him to call you back?" she asked. The return phone call was from the expert she had mentioned. At first, he seemed a bit suspicious. After explaining the precarious position of the well-intentioned graduate research team, he seemed a little more open to discussing our problem.

The problem the team had encountered was carefully explained. The confusing numbers and all of the tricks that were played to disguise the actual data were explained. After listening for a while, the expert casually said, "I have just completed a study of every field in the Soviet Union and I have all of the information you are attempting to find." As he continued, he also explained that he could not release the information to an outside third party. It seems that the information was classified as "top secret" by the US government. He did state that he could release the information if the party to receive it was approved by certain people within the US government.

By this time, the team was confused as well as elated. We had miraculously found the information, but it was classified, meaning we could not get it. The story about how an American oil expert was asked to do research on Russian oil fields is equally confusing.

It seems that the Russian government wanted a detailed study of the country's oil reserves, but they did not trust their own geologists. They sought out and hired someone that was recognized in the area to come in and analyze all of the fields in the USSR (our expert). They apparently felt that the security risk was reasonable since they believed that they needed an accurate assessment of their reserves. Thus, they hired the American who was recognized as one of the top experts in the world.

The US government had gotten wind of the project and advised the expert that he had permission to do the work, as long as it was not made available to inappropriate sources (i.e. those lacking the appropriate need to know and security clearance). As a result, the information was available – just not to our team.

We made a call to our client to ask about security clearance at his company. To our surprise, it turned out that the geophysical branch had appropriate security clearance to be able to have access to information of the type we had found. Then it all began to make sense.

Our suspicion was that our client had been hired by the US government to get the information on the oil reserves of the USSR as part of a major treaty negotiation that was in process at the time. Part of the treaty under negotiation involved underground nuclear testing. By obtaining the actual depths and locations of each oil field, it would be possible for the US intelligence community to differentiate between actual nuclear tests and the use of nuclear charges to stimulate oil reservoirs. Our client, even though it was a geophysical company, obviously had all of the security clearances needed to obtain the report that we had discovered.

Payback time

The day came for the final presentation to the client. This particular research team was made up of some real characters, so the decision was made to harass our professor a bit. The team began presenting each research area and the problems that were encountered in each one. As the story of each dead end was told, the professor would squirm just a little bit more with each story of failure. The team could see that he was getting to a point of low tolerance. As the team was summarizing all of the problems with the research and just how impossible the project was, the speaker handed the client the final report for the study. Included on it were the name, address, and phone number of the expert that had all of the information that the client needed. With that, a broad smile came over the professor's face.

KEY LESSONS

» Never give up. There is no substitute for persistence.

» Sometimes, clients are unable to tell you everything. Part of the intelligence process is to assume nothing.

» You can never predict where you will find your most important intelligence information.

» Trust no one. In the law enforcement business, they have a saying: "Believe half of what you see and none of what you are told." Good research is done by those who verify every aspect of their information.

CASE STUDY 3: MOTOROLA JAPAN

Low-power benchmarking

The following story was provided by Mark D. Stott, former manager of Motorola's intelligence unit. Often, American companies have little luck in obtaining intelligence information from foreign companies because they do not understand the culture of the country in which their information is domiciled. The following case provides an excellent demonstration of how one company used their knowledge of a country's culture to obtain intelligence information.

In the very early 1990s, the limited battery life of cellphones and pagers caused engineers and executives at Motorola to develop a task force dedicated to identifying the best sources of technology to resolve this issue. It was believed that far more phones and pagers would be sold and far more revenue generated for network operators if these products would last longer without recharging or replacing batteries.

A cross-functional task force was assembled to identify the current and potential future leaders in highly efficient rechargeable batteries and low-power semiconductors like linear power amplifiers and microprocessors. These were among the components that used the most power in radio designs and would have to be made more efficient to continue battery life gains.

In addition to looking at its own suppliers and those of competitors currently selling components for cellphones and pagers, the task force identified a set of companies developing components for other world-class portable electronics products like laptop computers, electronic organizers, portable CD players, and portable video games. Leading engineers at Motorola reasoned that these non-competitive products, many of which were being developed by vertically integrated Japanese multinationals, might well reflect faster rates of innovation because the markets and dollars affected were so much greater than the current cellphone market.

The problem was how to approach Japanese companies like Sony, Sharp, Casio, Toshiba, NEC, and Matsushita that were direct competitors in the cellphone market but had significant reason to co-operate with Motorola in identifying the best technology sources in the world for their very large consumer electronics businesses. Every culture has its right and wrong ways to be effective. In Japan, one of the little-known rules is that if a company president asks another company president in writing to arrange a meeting to discuss a topic, it is virtually required that the receiving party co-operate. The rules also say that an agenda should be provided by the requesting party at the time of the written invitation, outlining the specific topics that will be discussed. Lastly, the discussion needs to be an honest exchange of information, so the requesting company cannot expect only to ask questions without imparting comparable information.

Once the objectives were set out, Motorola chairman George Fisher agreed to send the letters to his counterparts at the Japanese multinationals. A 10-day window for the desired meetings was communicated with the exact schedule to be agreed later. With this approach, all of the Japanese companies mentioned above agreed to meetings between the key engineering and business unit personnel working on low-power semiconductors and a small cross-functional Motorola team. When the meetings occurred only one company, known for its closed culture, actually resisted supplying useful substantive information. By the end of the meetings, a thorough picture was developed of the technology road maps for both the portable consumer electronics manufacturers and the semiconductor suppliers one to five years in the future.

As a result of this picture, it was possible to project who the leaders would be in each category, when they expected to arrive there, and how long it would be before volumes would become significant enough to drive down costs for other customers like cellphone users. Basically, Sony and Sharp would be leading the way by introducing 3.3V semiconductors within the next year and moving to 2.2V products within a few more years. Watchmakers like Casio were already using components in the 1.1V range for their watches, and had the most experience at levels where the technology was expected to be the same very soon.

This information also helped Motorola decide where it could leverage other companies' efforts to push for earlier development of products needed sooner for cellphones. As a result of this well-executed intelligence effort, the firm's strategy was modified to fit expected changes in the competitive landscape.

KEY LESSONS

» Understanding your competitor can provide valuable insights into how effective intelligence can be obtained.

» In conducting global intelligence analysis, "cultural filters" and customs must be understood if an effective strategy for completing the assignment is to be developed.

CASE STUDY 4: APPLE COMPUTER

Using intelligence to develop a competitor profile

In early 1997, I was challenged by an associate to develop a strategic profile of Apple Computer and to predict future competitive moves of the organization. At the time, John Sculley had just resigned as CEO and there was speculation that Steve Jobs would return to take the position of CEO. There were a number of challenges associated with the research. To begin with, the company had been through a lot of turmoil over a period of years. One of the challenges was to discover the current state of the company. Another challenge was that of finding an appropriate group of experts to interview. They had to be knowledgeable about the inner workings of the company.

In order to profile the company, as well as predict future earnings, I chose the Ansoff model. I also used the Five Personalities of Change[1] assessment that I had developed to predict CEO behaviors.

The Ansoff model involves two broad areas: the future environmental turbulence and the current organizational profile. The environmental turbulence prediction involves research into future levels of innovation and marketing turbulence in the target segment. It also involves the use of a five-point scale, using an index of 1 to 5. Low levels of competition, product turn, and technological change are rated in the 1 range. As competition becomes more aggressive and the rate of change increases, the index will be in the 3 range. When the levels of innovation and marketing become overwhelming (i.e. highly chaotic with extremely fast rates of change), the turbulence will be in the 5 range. Normally, the turbulence will not be an even number, but will fall in some middle area. In the case of the future turbulence of Apple Computer predicted for the year 2000, the level was 4.4. At that turbulence level, product life cycles are quite short, competition is highly aggressive, and technological change is extremely fast.

The next step involves developing a profile of the company. The same five-point scale is used. At that time, eight broad attributes of the firm were measured. (I have since modified the model to assess 12 broad attributes, which are subdivided into 47 further attributes.) The eight broad attributes that were measured were:

1 marketing aggressiveness: the level of sales, advertising, and PR aggressiveness (at level 1, there would be no sales, advertising, or PR; at level 5 it would be extremely aggressive);
2 innovation aggressiveness: the company's aggressiveness in creating new products (R & D);
3 management: the leadership style and values of the firm's leaders (this ranges from highly controlling/risk-averse to highly empowering/risk-seeking);
4 culture: the internal culture of the organization, including reward systems;
5 structure: the formal structure of the organization;
6 decision systems: the speed of decisions and the level of use of early warning systems;
7 strategic planning: the planning model used by the firm (at level 1, the firm uses a linear planning model; at level 3 and above a non-linear model is used); and

8 strategic capacity: the number of staff and general management capable of doing creative strategic work.

As already stated, each attribute of the firm is rated on the five-point scale. This provides the analyst with the ability to compare the firm's present strategic profile with a future environment. (It should be noted that I have used this approach numerous times with a very high level of accuracy in predicting the future turbulence.)

Next, the analyst assesses the differences, or "gaps," between where the firm is currently positioned and where it needs to be in the future (as defined by the future turbulence). Those differences (if left uncorrected) have proven to have an impact on the future profit of the firm. For example, if turbulence is at level 4.4 and the management is at level 2 (a gap of -2.4), left uncorrected this would have a serious impact on the future profit of the firm. A chart of Apple Computer (Fig. 7.1) will explain the approach clearly.

The information needed for this study was obtained in accordance with the ethical standards of the Society of Competitive Intelligence Professionals. In addition to utilizing databases, a modified Delphi panel was used. Rather than using the traditional Delphi approach of revisiting with the experts a number of times for the purpose of obtaining unanimity, a single pass was used. The experts were interviewed regarding each attribute and, as a result, it was possible to eliminate dissenting opinions based upon the level of knowledge of the respondent. Generally, the experts all had a similar opinion of the future market (turbulence) of the industry.

The interviews with the experts proved extremely helpful. Once they gave their view of each aspect of Apple, each expert was encouraged to provide support for their view. By asking leading questions, it was possible to obtain some extremely valuable information. Normally, expert access can be obtained as long as the researcher understands that the expert's hourly fee must be met. The willingness to recognize the respondent's expertise creates a willing, helpful respondent.

The analysis

One of the difficulties in conducting the analysis had to do with the CEO. As mentioned above, John Sculley had just left the company at

Attribute	1	2	3	4	5	Profit impact
Marketing		X				Critical
Innovation			X			Serious
Management		X				Critical
Culture			X			Critical
Structure			X			Serious
Decision systems	X					Critical
Strategic planning	X					Critical
Strategic capacity				X		Matched

4.4   Future turbulence (2000)

Fig. 7.1 Apple Computer 1997 (Adapted with permission from H.I. Ansoff and E. McDonnell, *Implementing Strategic Management*, 2nd edn, Prentice Hall International (UK), Hertfordshire, 1990).

the time and the rumor was that Steve Jobs was on the way back in, at least as interim CEO. This, after Jobs had left the firm in 1985, when Sculley engineered the taking away of all of Jobs's responsibilities.

In looking at the Five Personalities of Change model (which has to do with predisposition toward change, and focus), Sculley and Jobs were at different ends of the scale. Jobs is what I call a Pathfinder personality and Sculley an Organizer.[2] Pathfinders are rare people, only 2.5% of the population. They are highly creative people who thrive on change. At the same time, they are usually horrible in senior management positions. They lack the desire to focus upon the daily operational and quality issues that give the organization stability. The Organizer, by contrast, is great at making an organization operate. However, they are highly resistant to change, and have a great deal of difficulty in processing dissonant data.

Under Sculley's leadership, Apple Computer became a stale bureaucracy. My interviews with experts familiar with Apple's condition in 1997 told me that the company had lost its creative intellectual capital (i.e. its key creative people). Further, the firm had become a compliance-based, risk-averse organization. Steve Jobs, in spite of his creative genius, was unable to recognize that the firm had to enter the PC market as well as stay in its current Mac market. This put the firm in a position of limited potential.

The return of Jobs (which had not happened at the time of the analysis) would mean that the firm would again become somewhat creative in developing new products. Sculley's departure meant that the operational stability would deteriorate. Steve Jobs's inability to see past his own creation into the PC market meant that the firm would be limited if he returned as CEO. Later, of course, he did return and was able to recreate the firm partially.

The analysis reveals that the company had numerous serious and critical profit-impact gaps. Marketing aggressiveness was low and even though the firm had some excellent products, the market was generally unaware of them. The experts agreed that the firm needed to be willing to innovate "out of the box" into the PC arena. The limited nature of the firm's innovation aggressiveness reveals some of this problem.

Critical gaps in management (highly controlling), culture ("don't rock the boat"), and strategic planning (linear thinking) further limited the firm's ability to enter a true reinvention stage. Although some interim innovations did allow the firm to grow its market share, the prospects for the firm remain limited in 2001 due to the continuation of the problems revealed in the diagnosis.

Using competitor profiles

From a competitive intelligence standpoint, using Ansoff-based strategic profiles can be extremely powerful. The profile clearly identifies a competitor's profit barriers and will help a firm's management understand how the competitor is most likely to assert itself in the market. Since the strategic profiles of competitors also predict the future profitability of the firm, that information can also be quite helpful to management. The nice thing about competitor profiles is that they are easily obtainable through databases and industry experts.

KEY LESSONS

» The more powerful the assessment model, the more powerful the output of the model.
» Even the most intimate information about a company is obtainable if you know who to ask.

CONCLUSION

As the case studies show, intelligence is more often focused upon predictive analysis than understanding current competitor behavior. Certainly, current behaviors may be helpful, but it is the predictive aspects of intelligence analysis that provide critical knowledge to the firm's strategy process. As previously stated, no two projects are identical. Conversely, the need for gifted, insightful, and tenacious intelligence analysts never subsides.

NOTES

1 Underwood, J. (1995) "Making the break: From competitive analysis to strategic intelligence," *Competitive Intelligence Review*, Vol. 6, No. 1. John Wiley & Sons, New York.
2 Ibid.

Key Concepts and Thinkers

There have been a number of people who have had an impact on the practice of intelligence. This chapter discusses these people, along with a number of intelligence concepts.

The intelligence community is replete with bright and capable people. The purpose of this chapter is to provide a brief look at some of the people in the field who have made a significant contribution. At the same time, it is important to remember that the list is in no way exhaustive.

The intelligence field is one in which the existence of "key concepts" is somewhat questionable. The reason is that a lot of concepts have been modified by practitioners, so that a term may have somewhat different meanings to different people.

There are numerous concepts associated with the field of intelligence. The concepts presented below are purposely limited to those that have the most importance at the current time. For a comprehensive look at concepts and definitions, see Fuld and Company's online intelligence dictionary (www.fuld.com).

AGAIN: WHAT EXACTLY IS *INTELLIGENCE?*

If the new definition of *management* is "the leading of organizational learning, transformation, and performance",[1] the critical role of the intelligence function in any organization becomes immediately apparent. Intelligence is at the heart of organizational learning and transformation. In Chapter 2, the following definition of *competitive intelligence* was offered: "Competitive intelligence is the identification of strategically important corporate intelligence (knowledge) needs and the process of resolving those needs through ethical information-gathering, analysis, and the presentation of such analysis to clients (internal or external)." In looking at the different terms used for intelligence processes, there are a number of issues that need to be understood. First consider the different phrases used to describe intelligence.

Competitive intelligence is used in a number of ways. For some, it might refer to understanding future moves of competitors. For others, it refers to the analysis of the present state of competitors, including their pricing, distribution, and products.

In some cases, the term *business intelligence* is used to differentiate it from military intelligence. In other cases, it can refer to a somewhat more broad view of the corporate intelligence process beyond just competitive issues.

Some suggest that *strategic intelligence* is different from *competitive intelligence* and *business intelligence*, because it supposedly involves a focus on the future. Others, including this writer, would disagree with that and suggest that all intelligence must focus on the future, since all other information is history. That is, it has already happened.

Some simply use the word *intelligence* interchangeably with all of the other terms. In a lot of ways, that may make the most sense. What you call the practice of intelligence is much less important than what is meant by the term.

KEY CONCEPTS

As suggested earlier in this book, the field of intelligence is currently being affected by a major paradigm shift that is occurring in the field of management and strategy. For over the previous 100 years, management theory had been based upon an economic theory called *equilibrium theory*. Around 1990, a number of management theorists began asking if the use of equilibrium theory-based models, which assumed a simplistic or linear model of the environment, was still appropriate. At the same time, the churn amongst companies listed on the Fortune 500 (an annual list of the top 500 US companies according to *Fortune* magazine) was evidence of the failure of the equilibrium-based, or linear-planning, approaches. During the 1990s, over 50% of the listing was eliminated and replaced by other companies.

A number of management theorists, in response to the apparent failure of the equilibrium-based models, began to investigate alternatives that explained the problems. A number found themselves looking at natural science and adopting ideas such as chaos theory and complexity theory. Ultimately, the idea of complex adaptive systems became popular. Underlying complex adaptive systems theory are the following two ideas.

1 The environment is complex as well as unpredictable, and therefore non-linear.
2 Darwinian evolution must be an appropriate metaphor for new management theory.

An intelligence book is not the place to resolve this debate (see *The Complexity Paradox*[2] in this series for full coverage), but there is a substantial basis for rejecting equilibrium-based thinking in favor of complex systems thinking when it comes to intelligence and intelligence tools. An overview of this topic is given in Chapter 6. With that said, the following are some of the key concepts used in the practice of intelligence. Some are clearly strategy tools that have been brought to the intelligence area. In a number of cases, comments will be offered regarding the usefulness or value of the concept.

Analysis–synthesis process

Analysis involves taking apart, while synthesis involves combining or boiling down. In actual practice, a three-step process (Fig. 8.1) can be extremely helpful to the analyst.[3] Experience has shown that most good intelligence analysts go through this process intuitively. In a lot of cases, they may make the leap from observation to application a bit too quickly. One way of adding discipline to the process is to complete each step sequentially, without allowing oneself to go to the next step until the previous one is complete.

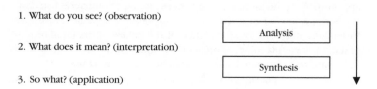

1. What do you see? (observation)

2. What does it mean? (interpretation)

3. So what? (application)

Analysis

Synthesis

Fig. 8.1 The three-step process of analysis–synthesis.

A disciplined look at "What do you see?" can lead the analyst to some interesting insights into the data. This is a form of data mining in that the observer is forced to go through data and simply list what they see. Often, the analyst will begin to see patterns or associations emerging. These patterns or associations can often tell a great deal about what is really going on.

Once the facts themselves are observed, the analyst enters the "What does it mean?" or analysis stage. An analyst may observe a pattern in a competitor's behavior that reveals purposeful misinformation prior to a new product release. In one client project, I observed a 10:1 ratio (difference) of articles and press releases favoring one future technology over another (regrettably, my client was on the short end of the ratio). As a result, I was able to explain to my client the problems the firm should expect in relation to customer expectations. The imbalance in the press had already created a very high awareness of the competing technology in the minds of the customers. This turned out to be a major issue for the client.

Once the data is analyzed and synthesized, it is important that the information be converted into a strategic meaning. Even though the information is synthesized into an understandable context, this does not mean that the executive who will read (or listen to) the report will necessarily understand how the intelligence is to be applied. In the case of my technology client, they needed to start a public relations, advertising, and publications initiative to win the hearts and mind of their customers. It would be impossible for them to win without changing the way the customers thought about the two different technologies.

Benchmarking

Benchmarking involves the idea of finding and copying a best-in-class practice or product. In the case of the Lexus automobile, the automaker assigned 500 engineers to study each component of the world's best automobiles and then design each component superior to the systems they had benchmarked.

From a practical standpoint, benchmarking has its value. But, as mentioned in Chapter 6, Gary Hamel and C.K. Prahalad have found that benchmarking can be misleading and wasteful. In a number of cases they found that companies' benchmarking activities had resulted in an out-of-date practice or product.

About three years ago, a major firm asked if I would conduct a benchmarking study for them. I agreed to do the study on a number of conditions. First, in addition to benchmarking key best-in-class organizations, I got the client's agreement to allow me to conduct a modified Delphi panel on the topic. Further, they agreed to allow me to study the future turbulence of the industry (see my title *Thriving in E-Chaos*[4] for a fuller explanation of this approach).

My client organization provided services for a number of different divisions of the company. A study of the future turbulence revealed that the environment would move to a turbulence level of 4.5 within three years (with 5 being the most turbulent). At that level of turbulence, there are extremely high levels of complexity, competition, and rates of change. This meant that my client organization had to be highly agile, even anticipating changes in how its services would be delivered to its internal clients. The first problem was that the client organization did not have the leadership style, culture, technology tools, and intelligence systems to deal with such an environment.

The benchmarking study revealed some important practices at a number of best-in-class companies. Prior to working with the Delphi experts, a number of literature searches were conducted to gather information about industry practices. From that, the Delphi panel research instrument was developed. The modified Delphi panel revealed that many of the best practices in the industry were not really the best practices at all. They were just what the companies happened to be doing at the time.

The turbulence study, plus the strategic diagnosis of the organization, revealed the barriers to performance that the organization would face in the future turbulent environment. The Delphi panel revealed a number of ideal best practices. Once the practices of the organization were assessed, a comprehensive transformation plan was developed that would enable the organization to deploy the best practices for the environment the firm would be operating in.

SWOT analysis

SWOT (strengths, weaknesses, opportunities, and threats) analysis first became popular in the strategy arena. Since it was introduced, it has been adapted to almost every area of management practice, including intelligence. SWOT is a form of environmental scanning that comprises internal and external scanning. Internal scanning involves an assessment of an organization's strengths and weaknesses. External scanning involves an assessment of opportunities and threats.

SWOT is an equilibrium-based, linear tool. As a result, it has many of the problems that relate to any simple process that is used in complex, dynamic environments. SWOT is often used to identify a firm's core competencies, which are then used to develop the firm's mission (i.e. the areas where the firm has competencies and the boundaries outside of which the firm is unable to compete).

Again, it is important to note that SWOT has lost most of its appeal according to complex systems theory advocates. However, one intelligence expert suggests a slight compromise: "It's a good tool to use for a first pass."

The intelligence community has made extremely good use of SWOT analysis as a competitor analysis tool. It does lack predictive power as it is designed, but a number of intelligence practitioners have developed processes for using the tool in a more predictive manner.

Strategic profiling

Strategic profiling, as exemplified by Table 7.1 in Chapter 7, is non-linear and can be much more powerful. The vertical line in the graphic represents the future turbulence that Apple Computer would face in the year 2000. The turbulence also reveals the level of aggressiveness and responsiveness that would be required of each attribute of the firm if Apple was to maximize profit in the future. The strategic profile of each attribute of Apple is revealed by the X on the chart. The further from future turbulence each attribute is, the higher the impact on future profit if the deficiency is not corrected. This approach, developed by H. Igor Ansoff, is the ultimate in gap analysis.

Not only can strategic profiling be used to predict the future earnings of a company, it is extremely useful in predicting future competitor behavior. In the case of Apple before Steve Jobs returned as CEO, there were numerous critical profit-impact gaps that would kill profitability if not corrected. The return of Steve Jobs corrected a number of the gaps.

CEO profiling

CEO profiling is another extremely important intelligence tool. Again, turbulence can be important in looking at the CEO. Notice that the higher the turbulence, the more charismatic and change-proactive the CEO must be (Table 8.1). Most companies in the global environment of 2001 are competing at turbulence levels of 4 to 5. An analysis of John Chambers (Cisco), David Novak (Tricon Global Restaurants, Inc., including Pizza Hut, KFC, and Taco Bell), and Dave House (Bay

Table 8.1   CEO attributes.

Factor	Level				
	1	2	3	4	5
Attitude toward change	Reject	Resist	Slow adaption	Drive change	Aggressively drive change
Attitude toward creativity	No value	Devalue	Necessary evil	Drive creativity	Aggressively drive creativity
Attitude toward subordinates	Expect performance	Expect efficiency	Meet objectives	Respect and value	Encourage as team member

Adapted with permission from H.I. Ansoff and E. McDonnell, *Implementing Strategic Management*, 2nd edn (Hertfordshire, Prentice Hall International (UK), 1990).

Networks/Nortel Networks) reveals that all three leaders will profile in the 4.5 range. It is my suspicion that Lou Gerstner (IBM Corporation) would profile in the same way.

What does this mean from an intelligence standpoint? The CEO profile helps explain how the CEO will manage, and subsequently how the organization will behave. Bill Gates and Steve Ballmer (Microsoft) will profile in the same way. All of these people are ideally suited for highly uncertain, extremely competitive environments because their leadership approaches encourage creativity, risk-taking, and winning.

All of these executives possess a prime mover mentality. Often, in interviews, they will all express the same paranoia about someone getting to the future before they do, or discovering the next break-through product. Simply put: if a competitive CEO profiles in the 4–5 range, watch out!

Linear forecasting

Linear forecasting is the process of taking historical data and extending it in a linear manner as a way of predicting the future. In the 1960s and 1970s for example, most companies could count on annual sales increases in the 10% range and profit increases in the same percentage. The equilibrium-based theories, while they do not explicitly state it, assume that the future will be linear. That, of course, is at the heart of the idea of core competencies and competitive advantage. It involves the assumption that whatever the firm has done in the past (i.e. demonstrating its core competencies) will be valued by the customer in the future.

Non-linear forecasting

Non-linear forecasting is the process of using systems thinking (i.e. relating to complex dynamic systems), scenarios, future turbulence analysis, and war-gaming to develop an understanding of the nature of the future. The non-linear thinker will not assert that they can accurately predict the future. They will suggest that they can develop highly reliable inferences about the nature of the future. In approximately 100 major studies involving mostly Fortune 500 companies over the past nine years, the turbulence predictions of the studies supervised or conducted by this writer have been extremely accurate.

Scenario planning

Scenario planning (see *The Art of the Long View* by Peter Schwartz[5] for an excellent approach to scenarios) involves the use of various information sources about the future. This non-linear process begins with the identification of the various driving forces that the analyst believes will have the most impact on the future of the area under study. Often, the information is converted into multiple scenarios, such as worst-case, most likely, and best-case. The scenarios are then converted to a case, or story of how the scenario will play out. Then, the team may evaluate all three (or more) scenarios for the purpose of developing a synthesized most probable scenario or contingency strategies for each scenario. This is an extremely effective non-linear tool.

Delphi panels

Delphi panels were developed at the Rand Corporation for the study of uncertain futures. By using repeated sessions with six or more experts, the researcher attempts to get consensus on each aspect of the future area under study. This writer has used modified Delphi panels (using 8–10 experts, assessing the knowledge of each expert, and eliminating those views that appear to be questionable) to achieve very high levels of accuracy in predicting future issues. Both approaches seem to be very reliable if properly administered.

Resistance to change

Resistance to change is a term that describes the natural tendency of most people to reject dissonant or different data. It is closely tied to *paradigm blindness*, which is used to describe the difficulty that most people have in mentally processing information that does not fit their existing mental model. In the practice of intelligence, resistance to change and paradigm blindness have an extremely high impact on the effectiveness of the intelligence team if they are not effectively managed.

KEY THINKERS

Due to limited space, only a few key thinkers will be discussed, and those only briefly. A number of historically significant people will be mentioned, plus a few relative newcomers.

Jan Herring

No discussion of competitive intelligence would be complete, without beginning with Jan Herring. Jan was trained at the Central Intelligence Agency (CIA), and later decided to transfer his intelligence skills to the corporate sector. He is credited with designing and founding Motorola's intelligence function, which is recognized by many as the best in the industry. Jan continues to work in the intelligence area as a consultant and seminar leader.

Dr Ben Gilad

Dr Ben Gilad formerly served as an associate professor of strategy at Rutgers University. He is widely recognized as a leader in the theory and practice of the competitive intelligence field. He is a frequent speaker at corporate functions, and continues to serve as a consultant to major companies.

Leonard Fuld

Leonard Fuld founded the firm that ultimately became Fuld and Company, one of the leading global providers of intelligence consulting and training. Fuld is recognized as a pioneer in the field of intelligence, and Fuld and Company continues to provide consulting and training to major companies around the world.

Zane Markowitz and Jim McNaughton

One senior intelligence expert once commented to me: "Markowitz and McNaughton is one of the leading-edge firms in the intelligence industry." Zane Markowitz and Jim McNaughton founded the firm that has played a quiet, yet important role in the evolution of the intelligence industry. They were very involved in supporting the early work that led to the founding of the SCIP. They have also been known for hiring and training many bright people over the years. The firm has also been a leader in adapting some important non-linear analysis tools, such as Delphi panels, to the field of intelligence.

Estelle Metayer

A relative newcomer to the field is Estelle Metayer, founder of Canada's Competia (www.competia.com). Five years ago, this firm did not exist. In just a few short years, Competia has become the focus of many in the intelligence business, basically due to Metayer's ingenious ability to recognize opportunity and rapidly move toward it. The firm now provides numerous educational opportunities for intelligence professionals, as well as intelligence training and consulting in both Canada and the US.

George Friedman

George Friedman is another relative newcomer who is changing the way intelligence is done. Friedman's dot.com company STRATFOR, based in Austin, Texas, now boasts more than 100,000 recipients of its daily intelligence briefing.

The STRATFOR team combines lightning-fast communication, with global resources in just about every country in the world to provide highly reliable information to its corporate clients. Although, as the STRATFOR team has discovered, their clients include more than just corporations. Included are a number of governmental agencies and embassies around the world.

The Intelligence Edge: How to profit in the information age is a hard-to-find, yet insightful book that was written by George, his wife Meredith Friedman, and some of the STRATFOR team.[6] STRATFOR has been widely recognized for its accurate and insightful predictions of world events over the past years.

Michael Sekora

Michael Sekora is also a key thinker and practitioner in the intelligence community. As the head of Project Socrates in the Reagan administration, Sekora became aware of the extensive amount of industrial espionage that is conducted by some countries against the industries of other countries. Sekora has taken his knowledge and now consults with large organizations in helping them defeat those who would attempt to gain access to their trade secrets illegally. Sekora's firm, Technology Strategic Planning, Inc. (www.tspinc.net) is located in Austin, Texas.

CONCEPTS, THINKERS, AND MORE

Space limitations simply did not allow for adequate mention of all of the great intelligence thinkers or emerging intelligence concepts. Intelligence is a field that is undergoing rapid change. As the global environment becomes more and more challenging, the ability to effectively gather and analyze intelligence will become increasingly important to the survival of organizations.

NOTES

1 Underwood, J.D. (2001) *Thriving in E-Chaos*. Prima Publishing, Roseville, CA.

2 Underwood, J.D. (2002) *Complexity and Paradox*. Capstone, Oxford.

3 Those familiar with biblical hermeneutics will be familiar with this process.

4 Underwood, *Thriving in E-Chaos.*

5 Schwartz, P. (1991) *The Art of the Long View: Scenario planning – protecting your company against an uncertain future.* Doubleday/Currency, New York.

6 Friedman, G. *et al.* (1997) *The Intelligence Edge: How to profit in the information age.* Crown, New York.

Resources

The evolution of the Internet and the availability of expanded databases have produced an information explosion for the intelligence analyst. This chapter discusses some of the most useful Websites and databases.

The intelligence community is global in nature. The emergence of the World Wide Web as an information repository has changed the nature of intelligence activity. In many cases, searches on the Web produce an overload of information that can in turn have the effect of making the intelligence analyst's job more difficult. Additionally, the Internet allows intelligence firms to serve clients around the world. Distance is no longer a barrier between a consultant and global markets. Furthermore, the emergence of numerous databases on the Web has had a major impact upon the business. This chapter will focus upon the more visible resources available.

The field of intelligence is rich in resources of almost every type and description. The explosion of the World Wide Web has not only removed national boundaries for competition, but has further provided immediate access to a wealth of global intelligence and information. The resource base for intelligence is massive. One need only do a Web-based search on a topic to begin to understand the infinite number of links that exist on almost any topic. In some cases, the analyst seems to be unable to find a final stopping point. In a lot of cases, entire "virtual knowledge" communities have sprung up on the global information highway. Once the analyst moves from free resources to fee-based resources, the base of information expands again. In most cases, in the electronic media area alone, the analyst can be overwhelmed. But that is just the beginning.

The need for third-party intelligence consultants has also caused the industry to grow at a rapid rate. With a steady supply of intelligence professionals from the military and government establishment, the level of professionalism and the development of enhanced methodology have grown too. Another factor that has contributed to the growth in the intelligence community has been the increasing level of industrial espionage that has been sponsored by a number of country-based government-industry intelligence organizations. As a result, organizations find themselves faced with the challenge of not only gathering effective intelligence, but also of protecting their intellectual capital from sometimes unscrupulous intelligence organizations.

Either way, it has become obvious to most organizations that there is a clear need for an effective intelligence program if a firm is to maintain its competitiveness. Just as the gathering of intelligence is crucial to an organization's future profitability, so the protection of existing knowledge has also become an imperative. The resources for doing both have become sophisticated and complex.

ORGANIZATIONAL RESOURCE OPTIONS

When it comes to the various resources for gathering and analyzing intelligence, there are a number of options available. Based upon financial resources and organizational size, it is possible to design an intelligence function for almost any organization. There are three basic ways in which the firm can organize the gathering and analysis of intelligence:

1 using an internal intelligence team;
2 using external intelligence consultants; and
3 using a hybrid intelligence system.

In the case of a very small organization, the creation of a small intelligence function may be all that the company can afford. In a lot of cases, the intelligence responsibility will be a small part of an individual's job. In most situations involving small companies, it may be difficult for the organization to justify the subscription costs for one of the private database vendors. In such a case, the intelligence analyst will be limited to secondary data that is available in industry publications and the Internet.

Some firms may convince themselves that they do not need an internal intelligence team even if they can easily afford it. These firms will often resort to utilizing external intelligence consultants on an as-needed basis. There are a numbers of advantages to this approach. First, the company only spends money when it identifies a clear need for intelligence. There is no need to have full-time intelligence staff on hand. Second, external consultants will be able to gather information (and conceal the firm's identity) more effectively if they are acting as a third party, versus a competitor. Third, external consultants are not subject to the internal biases and political pressures that an internal team would encounter.

A third way of setting up the intelligence function is by using a hybrid system. This involves having a full-time intelligence team and also the utilization of external consultants. This may be the most preferable way of organizing the intelligence function. There are a number of reasons why this is true.

1 The firm can more easily justify the required staff to meet the ongoing intelligence needs of the company.
2 The external consulting team can be used to test internally developed hypotheses, so that internal bias is prevented.
3 The firm is provided with a significant intelligence capability in the event that major demands hit the organization.
4 The hybrid system helps in selling the intelligence. It's one thing if the internal personnel bring in information that is unfavorable to the company. It's better if that same information is conveyed by an outside source as well.

Another resource decision the firm has to make has to do with information sources. Each resource is going to have different levels of cost. Some might disagree with the presentation in Fig. 9.1. It is important to remember that five areas determine the reliability of intelligence. These are:

Fig. 9.1 Information sources: quality and cost.

1 the quality and reliability of the source;
2 the quality and reliability of the information;
3 the depth and breadth of information gathered;
4 the methodology used in developing and analyzing the research; and

5 the researcher (knowledge, tenacity, and intuitive and analytical skills).

In terms of the relation of each area to reliability, it is important to observe that the cost generally increases as the quality increases. Consultants that can demand (and get) $5000–10,000 per day are able to charge that amount for a reason. Generally, clients find that they get relatively more value from the information obtained from a high-priced consultant than that obtained from a much lower-priced consultant. (This is not always true, of course, but it generally holds true.) The same is true of intelligence. The higher the level of expertise and the more sophisticated the analytical models utilized, the higher the cost.

From a practical standpoint, the organization that is considering starting an intelligence function needs to consider these issues. Another issue that must be understood is the bottom-line value of the intelligence. To put it another way, those planning the intelligence function must understand how intelligence can impact the firm's bottom line. This consideration must include the *intelligence opportunity cost* or the cost to the firm if the intelligence is not gathered.

SCIP

There is, perhaps, no organization that has done more for the practice of its discipline than the Society of Competitive Intelligence Professionals, or SCIP as it is known. SCIP was founded in 1986 with 300 members. Originally, the organization was focused upon local chapter meetings and creating an awareness of the value of intelligence in the business community.

By 2001, SCIP had become a global organization of over 7000 members, with a vast array of services for the global intelligence community. The services provided by SCIP are designed not only to enhance the level of professionalism in the industry, but also to link those in need of training or consulting with the very best in the profession.

Need a consultant? The SCIP Website (www.scip.org) can help you find the expertise you need by country or area. The search also gives important information about the different firms that work in the area and their specific areas of expertise.

Training is another area in which the organization is excellent. For professionals in the field, SCIP retains leading-edge practitioners to offer the latest in practice. For the new intelligence analyst, there is also appropriate training to bring them up to speed.

SCIP publications are another vehicle that the organization provides to help intelligence organizations enhance their professionalism. The bimonthly magazine is a practice-oriented publication that includes articles written by members. The *Competitive Intelligence Review* is a peer-reviewed research journal that includes articles and case studies.

There are other services like employment listings and chat rooms that encourage the exchange of ideas. The organization also maintains an online bookstore that features the latest and greatest, plus some of the classics, of the intelligence industry. The bottom line is that this organization is the focal point of the profession and has had a lot to do with the furthering of the intelligence field.

DATABASE RESOURCES

Over the pasts few years, the Web has changed drastically. The number of free, high-quality information sites has grown substantially. From an intelligence standpoint, it is important to remember that each provider will give access to the same information. At the same time, each will offer a small slice of information that is different from that offered by others.

In doing a first pass or more general search on a topic, there are two very good sites that provide information. The first is Google (www.google.com), which is a straightforward, dependable search engine providing some solid search capabilities. The second is Mamma (www.mamma.com), which markets itself as ''the mother of all search engines'' – to some extent its publicity holds true. Both of these sites are excellent starting points.

Once a broad search has been completed, it is then time to begin narrowing the search. One of the most comprehensive sites is About (www.about.com). It is surprising to discover the level of detail and the breadth of information that is available on this site. For example, many have never heard of LMDS (local multipoint distribution service). A simple search for LMDS will lead the researcher to a myriad of sources from which to gather information about LMDS.

A really interesting site is Brint (www.brint.com). An online search of Brint for LMDS reveals an extensive availability of important information. Brint also provides a fairly high level of technical detail in some of the sources it cites.

There are three excellent resources in the form of articles on the Competia site (www.competia.com). The first is an article by Estelle Metayer and Kristina Tomaz-Young titled "Competitive intelligence in Europe." The second is "European market research sources and expertise on the Internet" by David Mort. The third is "CI for the non-financial analyst: Part I" by Samuel Dergel.

Another useful site is Docere Intelligence (www.docere.se/english/news/world_ex.htm). This is loaded with information about global resources for the CI professional.

The next level for the researcher involves two sites. The first is called the CI Resource Index (www.bidigital.com/ci/Companies/Information/Business_Information/). This exceptional site provides the researcher with a number of key resource sites, and gives a detailed explanation of the information that is available on each site. This is an excellent resource for the intelligence professional. The other site that is extremely valuable is called Searcher (www.infotoday.com/searcher/feb99/lanza.htm). This leads us to an article by Sheri R. Lanza, president of Global InfoResources, Inc., titled "Around the world in 80 Sites: international business research." Lanza basically covers everything you ever wanted to know about business databases in her article. The article includes governmental as well as private free and fee-based resources. She also provides helpful insights into many important details about each resource.

The last stop for the researcher is the full range of fee-based resources, such as Dialog (www.dialog.com), Lexis-Nexis (www.lexis-nexis.com), Dow Jones (www.dj.com), DataStar (www.datastarweb.com), and Factiva (www.factiva.com). These are the resources that are most familiar to the intelligence community. Again, there are differences between each database, albeit often minor, that the researcher needs to be familiar with.

OTHER RESOURCES

The SCIP Website makes many of the better publications available at its online bookstore. There are many excellent books on the topic of intelligence, but there are two recent books that should be in every manager's library. I use the word *manager* because managers in almost every functional area of the firm need to be aware of the intelligence function and what it can provide the firm.

The first book is titled *Competitive Intelligence* by Larry Kahaner.[1] This book provides a nice broad look at the intelligence profession. It discusses a lot of mainstream practices along with some fairly leading-edge issues. This book is especially suitable for new intelligence personnel. It contains much "intelligence wisdom." Its many insights are of use to anyone interested in the intelligence profession.

The second book is more appropriate for experienced intelligence professionals. It is titled *Proven Strategies in Competitive Intelligence* and edited by John E. Prescott and Stephen H. Miller.[2] The book contains a series of articles by some exceptional intelligence professionals. One article in particular involves some extremely important knowledge that could be quite helpful for companies competing in highly competitive, turbulent environments. The article "Scenario analysis and early warning systems at Daimler–Benz Aerospace" by Franz Tessun is insightful at a minimum.

As strategic theory moves past equilibrium theory (linear modeling) into complex systems theory (non-linear modeling), the use of non-linear complex systems tools is becoming extremely important. Over the last three years, in supervising work by graduate research teams as well as doing my own consulting work for major companies, almost every strategic diagnosis has indicated a need for an early warning system. (In every case the client was a Fortune 500 firm.)

There are many good books available on the topic of competitive intelligence. The two books mentioned are simply great books to have as resources. For the serious learner in the field of intelligence, a tour of the bibliographies of the two books, plus a tour of the SCIP online bookstore, is strongly recommended.

NOTES

1 Kahaner, L. (1996) *Competitive Intelligence: From black ops to boardrooms – how businesses gather, analyze, and use information to succeed in the global marketplace*. Simon & Schuster, New York.

2 Prescott, J.E. and Miller, S.H. (eds) (2001) *Proven Strategies in Competitive Intelligence: Lessons from the trenches*. John Wiley & Sons, New York.

Ten Steps to Making it Work

This application-oriented chapter provides a clear map for designing and managing an effective intelligence organization.

Due to the fact that every intelligence project may be significantly different from any other, the key in developing an effective process centers on speed and flexibility. There are, however, specific keys to ensuring the success of an intelligence function.

Each industry may have specific issues that need to be addressed in different ways. Generally, the 10 steps suggested in the following will ensure that a program achieves long-term success.

1. ENSURE CEO SPONSORSHIP OF THE INTELLIGENCE TEAM

Having CEO sponsorship is the first, and most important, step in developing a successful intelligence program. In some cases, companies have put research and intelligence functions in such strange places as the finance department. Generally, that is a formula for failure. In other cases, the function is domiciled in the marketing department. That is preferable, but may still lead to problems.

Intelligence organizations need stability. They cannot be formed, disbanded, and then effectively reformed without negatively impacting the quality of the department. As most corporate intelligence people will tell you, there are always those in an organization who see the intelligence budget as one of the first expenditures that the company can eliminate.

CEOs tend to be extremely busy people. Giving them the responsibility of supervising the intelligence organization is not something that will usually have even CEO support. At the same time, if the intelligence organization does not report directly to the CEO, the department will often become lost in the internal political activities of the organization. Additionally, if the team does not report directly to the CEO, that often results in filtering of intelligence information. That is, those supervising the intelligence process might be tempted to avoid sending unfavorable information to the CEO so as to hide organizational deficiencies.

These problems also create others for the intelligence organization. Specifically, they create resource problems. The intelligence organization needs to have access to the firm's brightest people. If the department is seen as a political football, subject to every budget-cutting whim of the annual planning process, the people the intelligence organization needs will be unwilling to work in the area.

It usually gets down to the simple reality that the intelligence team must be CEO-sponsored. In other words, not only must the team have the CEO's proactive support, but it must also report to the CEO. Additionally, it means that the senior intelligence manager must also be recognized in key corporate activities. The senior intelligence manager needs to have periodic briefings with the CEO. More importantly, the organization needs to know that. Further, the senior intelligence manager needs to be included as part of the key strategy team within the organization. All of these activities send a message to the organization about the commitment to the intelligence function.

2. SELECT THE RIGHT PEOPLE FOR THE INTELLIGENCE TEAM

The creation of an effective intelligence organization requires the right personnel selection for the group. The truth is that some people have an aptitude for intelligence work and others have absolutely none. In Chapter 7, the Five Personalities of Change model was discussed. Table 10.1 summarizes the characteristics of each personality.

The table describes in order each personality. In reality, my work with assessments of personnel indicates that most people have at least two predispositions, a primary and a secondary. It is important to remember that the basic predisposition is not something that can be changed. Thus, it is important to understand each personality and how to effectively link each one in order to maximize the intelligence effort.

In selecting personnel for an intelligence team, it is important to ensure that those with a primary Pathfinder personality be selected first. Since Followers and Patriots dislike change (and therefore dissonant information), these personalities should be segregated off the team. In addition to Pathfinders, a number of Listeners and a few Organizers are necessary.

A few years ago I did a seminar in Canada for a telecommunications provider. As a part of the seminar, I administered a Five Personalities assessment that I had developed with an associate A few weeks later, I received a call from one of the participants. He asked permission to

Table 10.1 The Five Personalities of Change model.

Personality	Characteristics	Attitude towards change
Pathfinder (2.5% of population)	Sees without bias; inquisitive; a first learner	Discovers the future
Listener (13.5% of population)	A mediator; a bridge between Pathfinder and organization	Little resistance toward change
Organizer (34% of population)	Typical, driven manager-type personality	Fairly resistant to change
Follower (34% of population)	Stability-oriented; dislikes Pathfinder	Highly resistant to change
Patriot (16% of population)	Narrowly focused; will fire Pathfinder if possible	Will sabotage change initiatives if possible; hates change

Sources: E.M. Rogers, *Diffusion of Innovations* (New York, Free Press of Glencoe, 1983) and J. Underwood, "Making the break: From competitive analysis to strategic intelligence," *Competitive Intelligence Review*, Vol. 6, No. 1 (New York, John Wiley & Sons, 1995).

use the assessment instrument with his research laboratory team in Ottawa. I agreed.

About a month later I received another call from the individual. He said that the assessment had revealed some powerful information. On those projects that had failed, they had put the wrong people in key positions. On the projects that had been most successful, they had the right personalities in the most appropriate roles. All of the placements had been randomly made on the projects he discussed. As a result, the team began using the Five Personalities assessment to place people on each project strategically. For example, their primary researchers needed to have a Pathfinder predisposition. Their project managers needed to have a primary Listener predisposition. The leaders of each team needed to have a primary Organizer personality, and a secondary Pathfinder predisposition. After using the instrument for over a year, the senior manager of the laboratory reported consistently positive results.

3. CREATE AN INTERNAL INTELLIGENCE SYSTEM

An effective intelligence function is based on an internal intelligence system. An internal intelligence system involves the creation of a formal system for involving every member of the firm in the intelligence process. This needs to be a system that is proactively supported and it must link every individual in the organization. This can be done in a number of ways, but normally the firm's existing network is the best way to do it.

In one case, a software company I worked with needed a way for all of its employees not only to share information, but also to work collaboratively in discussing the information. The firm had a new CEO at the time, and he recognized how important this process would be in taking the organization forward.

As a result, the firm deployed Lotus Notes and created a bulletin board concept for the posting of information. As one employee posted information, others were encouraged to comment or add information. Almost overnight, the processing and distribution of information within the firm exploded.

There is one important thing to remember. If an intelligence system is to be successful, every contribution must be acknowledged. Unless the contributors understand the value of their information, the flow will cease. Additionally, when someone makes a big discovery, there need to be ceremonial procedures in place so as to recognize the individual's contribution adequately in the eyes of the entire organization. The importance of ceremony and recognition cannot be overstated: it is critical to long-term success.

4. ALLOCATE A SUITABLE BUDGET FOR INTELLIGENCE WORK

The intelligence organization needs to have access to certain resources if it is to do its job effectively. First, in the normal course of business, the firm needs to have access to periodic industry reports. These are usually from one of the research firms, and are often somewhat lacking in specificity in relation to the firm. They are, however, important in helping the intelligence team to understand what competitors are thinking or planning.

A lot of intelligence organizations do not have a discretionary budget that allows them to retain outside experts periodically. Experts can provide extremely important information and be of critical importance in the intelligence-gathering process.

Another discretionary area involves retaining outside consulting firms. One might ask, "Why hire an outside consulting firm when we have our own intelligence organization in place? Doesn't that mean we don't need our internal intelligence team?" Outside intelligence consultants have three distinct advantages over the internal team.

1 In some cases, they may have individuals who possess knowledge that is important for a specific project.
2 Since they are an outside firm, they can gather information discreetly, without disclosing the identity of the firm that is gathering the information.
3 Since they are a disinterested third party (and not a competitor), they will be able to get better access to important sources in some cases.

Effective intelligence-gathering and security involves the ability of the intelligence team to hire outside consultants. Budgetary allocation for such projects is extremely important.

5. ROTATE KEY MANAGERS THROUGH THE INTELLIGENCE ORGANIZATION

Many companies have a career path program for high potential managers. In most cases, the fast-track employees are routed through the most important areas of the company in order to prepare them for their future responsibilities rapidly. By including a tour or duty in the intelligence group of the firm as part of their training, the individual gains an understanding of the value of the function.

6. GIVE THE INTELLIGENCE TEAM APPROPRIATE RESOURCES AND ACCESS

There are three very important resources that an intelligence team needs if it is to do its job well:

1 appropriate databases;
2 access to standards information and organizationally sensitive information; and
3 trade associations and conferences.

While access to all of the above may seem logical to some, in many cases internal intelligence teams are left out of the information loop.

All databases are not alike. Most good databases are expensive. Good intelligence work demands that the intelligence group have extensive access to various databases. Each database may have many of the same sources included. The problem is that most of them are not identical. That is, some will have included some sources that, while minor, may prove important to a specific project. So it is important for the researcher to have the ability to conduct an effective search, which may mean that the team may need access to multiple databases.

Frequently, there are standards groups that are composed of key technical personnel from different companies. In industries like wireless telecommunications, access to the negotiations between different companies regarding proposed standards could reveal a great deal about each company's strategy in the segment. The intelligence team needs to have access to the proceedings from such meetings.

Finally, the intelligence team needs to have a budget to cover attendance at various industry conferences and trade shows. It is not unusual for competitors at such meetings to reveal sensitive information inadvertently to get the customer's ear.

7. ESTABLISH A WAR ROOM

War rooms, or *situation rooms* as some call them, are a central repository for competitive information. The idea is to have a central location in which all databases can be accessed and also where recent research (e.g. concerning competitors' strategic profiles) is readily accessible.

There are those who would suggest that technology now makes virtual war rooms a reality. While this may be true, such statements fail to recognize the important role that the presence of the war room plays. The war room provides a focus for intelligence activities. It provides a common area of access for those who need the ongoing research of the intelligence team. Most importantly, the war room's presence sends a clear message to the organization about how senior management values the intelligence function. That is an extremely important message if a company is to have a sustainable organizational learning capability.

8. LINK A FIRM'S STRATEGY WITH ITS INTELLIGENCE FUNCTION

In an ideal situation, the intelligence team should be a major provider of information for the team that develops the firm's strategy. In many firms, however, the strategy process is little more than confirming that the firm will continue to do what it has done in the past (Ryall's "self-confirming theory"[1]). Normally, a great deal of activity surrounds such a process, but in the end the real strategy process is little more than budgeting activity.

In true learning organizations, strategy is complex, and non-historically focused. This means that those creating the strategy recognize their need to learn from others in the organization. Learning organizations are open systems, and as such understand the critical link between intelligence and strategy. In Chapter 1, I offered my definition of *management*: "the leading of organizational learning, transformation, and performance." Organizations in complex environments are continually becoming something different. Only effective learning can provide a basis for transformation. High performance is the result of the learning and transformation process. Thus, one of the keys for an effective intelligence function, and the sustaining of organizational learning, is to properly link the intelligence team with corporate strategy.

9. DESIGN THE INTELLIGENCE PROCESS TO FIT THE PROJECT

Once an intelligence team allows itself to sink into a "one size fits all" process, its work will deteriorate. At the same time, a flexible yet systematic intelligence process is extremely important. One of the problems relating to intelligence analysis is that in many cases analysts are not trained to design their process to fit the project.

Also, it is possible for an analyst to become too reliant on some of the off-the-shelf research reports. In Chapter 6, a process map for developing effective intelligence was presented. The process is designed to address two key issues:

1 clearly identifying the need the project is to meet, including the time and urgency requirements; and
2 managing the client and any resistance to change by using stage briefings at different points along the way.

In some cases, the intelligence team will get a project on Friday that needs to be delivered on Tuesday. The process needs to be flexible enough to adapt to these time schedules. This aside, in my opinion it's the upfront work that makes a project successful. If the client's needs and circumstances are not understood upfront (they often do not tell the whole story), the project can be doomed to failure from the start. A good example is a project that is handed over with a stated objective, when in actuality it's being done to resolve a dispute between two executives. With such projects, stage briefings can help an analyst to gain an understanding of what they are really dealing with.

10. USE STRATEGIC PROFILES TO FACILITATE ORGANIZATIONAL LEARNING

If organizational learning is truly to occur, a company with a strategic profile such as Apple Computer in 1997 (see Table 7.1 in Chapter 7) must change their profile or the intelligence will not be translated into learning. A leadership style that discourages risk and creativity, plus a culture that rewards compliance, will destroy any attempt to change the status quo.

The basic profile of Apple Computer in 1997 (prior to Steve Jobs's return) was one characterized by high levels of resistance to change, a political bureaucracy, and an inability to respond rapidly. In short, the organizational profile reveals that regardless of the intelligence information made available at that time, there was little if any chance that it would be heeded.

It is important to remember that it takes both hard systems (technology) and soft systems (leadership, culture, decision systems, etc.) to perform in highly complex, high-speed environments. A turbulence level of 3.7 or above means that the environment will be highly turbulent. An organization with profile aspects of 2 to 2.5 means that the firm is simply unable to handle either complexity or high rates of environmental change. In essence, it means that the firm is unable to process the information effectively in the first place.

A COMPLEX, INTERDEPENDENT PROCESS

As a sailboat racer, I know that winning races involves a lot of things. The fastest boat, without a solid crew, will not win a race. A fast boat, with a good crew that is lacking an excellent helmsman, will still not win. The same is true of the intelligence process in an organization.

It takes all of the complex aspects of a good intelligence system if the intelligence process is to yield positive results. Everyone in the intelligence business has had the experience of presenting a firm with information that was critically important (in some cases relating to the survival of the firm), only to have it rejected outright. Without the balance of the complex aspects that allow an intelligence system to function, there can be no success either for the intelligence team or for the firm.

NOTE

1 Ryall, M.D. (1998) "When competencies are not core: Self-confirming theories and the destruction of firm value." Working paper, William E. Simon Graduate School of Business Administration, University of Rochester.

Frequently Asked Questions (FAQs)

Q1: What is competitive intelligence?

A: Competitive intelligence is the identification of strategically important corporate intelligence (knowledge) needs and the process of resolving those needs through ethical information-gathering, analysis, and the presentation of such analysis to clients (internal or external).

Q2: Isn't competitive intelligence the same as industrial espionage?

A: Not at all. In fact, the professional intelligence community prohibits unethical behavior in the gathering of intelligence.

Q3: What's the big deal? Isn't competitive intelligence simply research?

A: In some ways, yes, it is simply research. However, good intelligence goes beyond research into providing reliable, actionable analysis for the recipient of the information.

Q4: Can everyone be an intelligence analyst?

A: Many people can do the work. However, it does take individuals with high levels of tenacity and intuition to do excellent intelligence work.

Q5: It looks like all that intelligence people do is run searches on databases or buy custom reports from outside providers. Is this true?

A: Some may do this, but this is not intelligence work. Gathering the information is just the first step toward effective analysis.

Q6: It seems like the only people who can afford an intelligence function are the Fortune 500. Is this the case?

A: No, even small companies can conduct effective intelligence studies. In a lot of cases, they may need the information just as much as large companies.

Q7: Why is competitive intelligence important?

A: It is important because it has to do with the future of your company, especially its profitability or even survival.

Q8: Don't some companies steal information from others? Is it possible to protect yourself?

A: Yes, theft is fairly common. In a lot of cases, companies do not know it has occurred until it is too late. It is possible to prevent most losses.

Q9: What is counter-industrial espionage?

A: Counter-industrial espionage involves preventing the activities of illegal or unethical individuals within your company.

Q10: Where does technology enter the intelligence picture?

A: Technology usually involves portals to the Internet. Unethical individuals use those portals to gain access to important corporate information.

Index